Motivating Every Student in Literacy (Including the Highly Unmotivated!) Grades 3–6

Sandra K. Athans & Denise Ashe Devine

EYE ON EDUCATION
6 DEPOT WAY WEST, SUITE 106
LARCHMONT, NY 10538
(914) 833–0551
(914) 833–0761 fax
www.eyeoneducation.com

Library of Congress Cataloging-in-Publication Data

Athans, Sandra K., 1958–

   Motivating every student in literacy, grades 3-6 : (including the highly unmotivated!) / Sandra K. Athans & Denise Ashe Devine.

      p. cm.

   ISBN 978-1-59667-121-8

   1. Language arts (Elementary) 2. Motivation in education. I. Devine, Denise Ashe, 1967– II. Title.

   LB1576.A78 2009

   372.6—dc22

                                                                                                    2009015413

10 9 8 7 6 5 4 3 2 1

Free Downloads

The motivation tools found in Appendix B of this book are available free for book buyers on the Eye On Education website. Anyone who has purchased this book has permission to download and print them out.

You can access these downloads by visiting www.eyeoneducation.com. Click on FREE Downloads, or search or browse our website to find this book's page and scroll down for downloading instructions. You'll need your book buyer access code: **MOT-7121–8**.

Contents

Preface

As classroom teachers, we've worked with real students in real classrooms for many years. We've also worked with numerous outstanding teaching professionals within our district. Many shared their vast years of successes and continued challenges with us, and allowed us to include their ideas in this book. In addition, we've strengthened our understandings of student motivation by working with teachers and educators while providing workshops and sharing experiences at regional and national conferences. Based on our own classrooms and the exchange of ideas from other hardworking, determined teachers, this book outlines our collective experiences working toward improving difficulties that stem from a lack of student motivation and effort.

Our discussions are from the point of view of *regular* classroom teachers. Our advice and recommendations are not intended to replace those of a medical provider or other professional from within or outside of the field of education. We have not excluded from our discussions students who might be receiving professional assistance or who have special academic accommodations. Moreover, most students—no matter a student's situation—will benefit in some way from the classroom-tried-and-tested methods described here. Still, we must express that caution be exercised and good judgment be used as you assume the task of coordinating professional information about your students with the information presented here. Likewise, you might also consider your own school and state policies regarding issues of student privacy, parental involvement, and any other requirements that might be needed for you to work with students in the manners suggested here.

We also wish to make clear that the case studies and classroom vignettes appearing throughout the book are composites that, although based on real experiences, have been used in place of actual case studies to assure confidentiality. Fictitious names have also been used throughout.

We hope these practical strategies and tools, which have proven successful for us, will benefit you in your classrooms. The ideas have withstood the test of time, and they have held up under data-based classroom study. Also, many incorporate *best-practice* ideals espoused by a spectrum of motivational and educational specialists and have undergone their share of scrutiny. More importantly, all have proven worthwhile to some of the toughest (yet most deserving) critics of all—real students.

We also hope you'll find some humor in the light-hearted comic-book designators—Superhero and Underdog Strategies—we've used to group and discuss the techniques appearing in the book. We all recognize the serious challenge and escalating urgency to address student motivation; still, interjecting some fun, a little of the fantastic, may be refreshingly uplifting. Lastly, we continuously struggle with the phrase "highly unmotivated," used often throughout this book, especially in Chapter 4, and clarify that we are not using the term to label a student or group of students. Rather, we use it to refer to *behaviors* that may be exhibited by a student or students; behaviors that are among the challenges that prevent student success.

Any Need For Background Knowledge in Literacy?

A unique feature of this work is that it links motivation and literacy together, offering a practical starting point to tackle a difficult issue. Terms that may be unique to the literacy field are explained and illustrated through examples, classroom vignettes, and case studies. There are no requirements for specific background knowledge. Likewise, it is not important that you follow our same literacy-based approach to instruction (discussed in Chapter 1). Many components of our approach are based on best practices and are undoubtedly already in place in your classroom.

Strengths and Unique Characteristics of this Book

Lack of motivation continues to be one of the most misunderstood and impenetrable barriers that cripples student success. This book offers many innovations that provide positive hope for change:

♦ Unique to this work is the connection between motivation and literacy which represents a starting point, a new opportunity and outlook to affect an ongoing problem.

♦ Case studies, vignettes (stories), models, and anecdotes—all from *the classroom*—make this a practical troubleshooting tool you can return to time and time again, as new needs arise. The main idea of each chapter is synthesized, allowing you quick review and easy-return access to areas that may prove helpful in the future.

♦ A *Motivation Improvement Action Plan* leads you step-by-step through a planning process as you incorporate and tailor *Tips* from the text into your own teaching activities. Also, each chapter begins with a reflection—typical classroom scenarios, a synthesis of relevant research, and other pertinent information that represent glimmers of timesaving insights—that will help guide you in your own planning.

♦ The work is grounded in the *best practices* of authorities in literacy and motivation and is also based on nearly ten years of classroom-based action research. Tools and strategies are all classroom tried and tested, and many were devised by classroom teachers.

♦ Differentiated plans for addressing motivation improvement for *all* students are provided ensuring that *all* students' needs are addressed. Outcomes for classroom case studies are provided in Appendix A. Classroom vignettes also describe scenarios to help convey the ideas or events explained in the text.

♦ Numerous tools and resources are provided, including student plans and contracts, charts, and more, all classroom ready and reproducible for classroom use.

Organization of this Book

Chapter 1, *Motivation and Literacy: A Vision for Success*, describes "The Quality Comprehension Model" and our experiences shaping this strategy-based reading approach. We also share our findings about the affects of motivation on student success and outline a process readers may wish to use to create a vision for improvement.

Chapter 2, *Superhero Strategies to the Rescue!*, features powerful strategies that can be integrated into your literacy-based activities and language arts curriculum. Often referred to as "process strategies," they blend into larger instructional processes and activities within a classroom.

Chapter 3, *Underdog Strategies to the Rescue!*, describes quick, easy-to-use "fixes" that can be used to interject novelty and variety into your curriculum. There is a place for these strategies alongside those that are more permanent and process driven.

Chapter 4, *Reaching the Highly Unmotivated*, offers strategies that, although helpful for many, are most effective with those students who struggle with pervasive motivational difficulties within literacy-based activities.

Chapter 5, *Frequently Asked Questions*, provides answers to questions we're typically asked during workshops and conferences.

Appendices provide a collection of resources for teachers to use. Appendix A, *Case Study Outcomes—Strengths and Remaining Challenges*, demonstrates how the strategies discussed in the book can be applied to real situations that occur in the classroom. Appendix B, *Reproducible Charts*, provides a blank version of your "Motivation Improvement Action Plan" (described below) together with classroom-ready charts, record-keeping devices, forms, and other aides that are reproducible and designed to be used by the classroom teacher.

Your Motivation Improvement Action Plan

Also included in this book is a "Motivation Improvement Action Plan," a step-by-step plan you devise to meet your own classroom needs. Using the "Motivation Tips" that are highlighted in many chapters, you can easily develop your plan by adding ideas and strategies as you encounter them in your reading. The plan is introduced in Chapter 1 and continues throughout the book. A sample plan is featured throughout to further guide you toward success. A reproducible plan for you to complete appears in Appendix B as a black-line master (you may wish to copy this before you begin your reading). Ways in which you might use the "Motivation Improvement Initiative Tips" for your own planning, as well as other discussions we hope are helpful, are also presented.

If you've picked up this book hoping to find some answers, a plan, or perhaps a little of both in your quest for improvement, we pass along these words to you in keeping with the spirit that enabled us to write it: *Use this book as you wish!* These are the words that we used as we passed materials back and forth, shared ideas, and helped each other troubleshoot solutions. They capture the collaborative spirit of our teacher-driven effort; they represent a teacher's version of *abracadabra* in a light-hearted, comic-book kind of way.

Meet the Authors

Sandra K. Athans is a fourth-grade teacher and has provided instruction at this level for nine years within the Chittenango Central School District in Chittenango, New York. She has also taught at the preschool level, the sixth grade level, and recently served as an adjunct professor within the English Department at Cazenovia College.

Having earned a Bachelor of Arts degree in English from the University of Michigan, Ann Arbor, Sandra entered the field of publishing where she worked in New York City and White Plains, New York. She excelled in this field for nearly ten years before pursuing a career in education. Sandra earned her Master of Arts degree in teaching from Manhattanville College, Purchase, New York, in 2000, and recently received her Secondary English Certification.

In addition to assisting students in her role as a classroom teacher, Sandra introduced and provided instruction in many engaging after-school programs that encouraged students' authentic reading and creative writing activities.

Motivating Every Student in Literacy is Sandra's second book and is based on her experience studying and working with intermediate-level students in the areas of guided reading, reading comprehension, and motivation. She has been awarded numerous grants through the Central New York Teaching Center and enjoys sharing her experience at reading and writing conferences throughout the United States.

Denise Ashe Devine received her Bachelor of Science in elementary education in 1989 and her Master of Science in reading from the State University of New York at Oswego in 1993. She has been teaching for just over 20 years and, in that time has provided instruction at various elementary grade levels within several school districts in the central New York area.

In addition to this experience, Denise was involved in a summer instructional program for at-risk students and their families. In this capacity, Denise provided reading instruction for elementary-level students and their parents. Denise also serves as the fourth-grade chairperson on the Chittenango Central School District's Elementary Curriculum Council, representing the curriculum concerns of all nine fourth-grade classroom teachers.

Over the past several years, Denise has actively been involved in researching critical issued in education, such as guided reading, comprehension, and motivation at the intermediate levels, and has been awarded numerous grants to study these topics. In addition to these roles, Denise is an active after-school instructor, offering creative programs in reader's theater and creative writing. Denise is also a frequent speaker at conferences and workshops throughout the United States. *Motivating Every Student in Literacy* is her second book.

Motivation and Literacy: A Vision for Success

Identifying a starting point doesn't necessarily imply there will be an end, but it gives us hope. Defining goals and establishing a tone will help guide your vision.

Does This Happen in Your Classroom?

Ms. Stewart sat together with six students at a small table near the back of the classroom. She glanced at the clock, keeping track that Mr. Evans, who provided remedial reading support services, would be finishing with his group of readers in twenty minutes. She had five more minutes with her first group and would then call her second group to the back. Juanita was sharing her summary of a passage from *Love that Dog*, which the students had read at the start of their small-group instruction. The students chuckled quietly, amused by Juanita's descriptive interpretation of the important ideas. Pleased with Juanita's progress and the others' level of engagement, Ms. Stewart glanced around the classroom, quickly assessing the progress of the eight other students who sat at their desks. They were involved in a variety of independent reading projects. It was clear that Steven had made little progress with his assignments; he was well behind the others and was flipping through pages of his book, expressionless. Caitlyn was busy inspecting different colored erasers in her pencil box. She quickly selected one, having spied Ms. Stewart watching her, and returned her box inside her desk. Ms. Stewart assumed Steven and Caitlyn would need to catch up on their reading activities in study hall during recess; this would be their third visit to study hall that week.

Although the names may be different, Stevens and Caitlyns are in every classroom and in every grade level. We recognize that each student is unique, yet we are all too familiar with the type of student who, for whatever reason, is unmotivated to work to his or her potential—we remember them.

Our studies into motivation began as a result of the countless episodes such as this one with Steven and Caitlyn. It was never our intention, but rather an incidental outcome of what we considered—at the time—a loftier goal. Initially, our objective was focused on our reading comprehension instruction. Our goal was to substantially improve the reading ability of *all* of our students. At the onset of this challenge, we identified best practices from authorities and shaped an instructional approach for reading comprehension that seemed to work well within our classrooms. By our seventh year, we were delighted that most of our students were making significant gains. Evidence supporting this was duplicated many times over; students' classroom performance on pre- and postinstruction benchmark assignments and tests showed strong growth, and the number of students passing our state language arts tests at proficiency levels or higher, was growing. Our success was invigorating. As we had hoped, our students were making substantial progress in reading comprehension skills—most of our students, that is… except for the Stevens and the Caitlyns.

Why Motivation and Literacy?

All too often, vague complaints resound that the Stevens or the Caitlyns simply are not using their best effort. These broad generalizations are just that, and they rarely serve as a workable beginning to address the much larger problems that stem from students who are disengaged and challenged by a lack of motivation. Being able to define student behaviors and performance in more concrete terms such as within the parameters of a literacy approach seemed like a well-defined beginning. In an article about critical thinking, Daniel T. Willingham contends that when trying to provide instruction on this elusive concept, success will be more readily forthcoming if its content is presented in a framework that makes use of it, such as the "Scientific Method" (Willingham, 2007). We found the same is true when trying to affect student motivation—it needs grounding.

Because the focus of this work is to improve student motivation within literacy-based activities—reading, writing, listening, speaking, viewing, and thinking—we begin by sharing a brief overview of our approach to reading comprehension instruction. This provides a context for subsequent discussions and also enables you to draw parallels to your own literacy activities. By doing so, you can determine how to make the best use of the suggestions in this book. We also provide prompts where you might wish to reflect on your classroom practices now that you're taking a fresh look at routine activities with a critical eye on student motivation. As mentioned in the *Preface*, it's not important that you follow our approach to reading comprehension instruction, yet we do highlight activities that research suggests are beneficial. Because of this, we are confident that many components of our approach will sound familiar and that many of them—in some shape and form—may already be in place in your classrooms. Also, the strategies and techniques introduced here can easily be integrated into other literacy-based activities.

Our Approach: The Quality Comprehension Model

Like all teachers who provide instruction to intermediate-level learners, we desperately hoped that our students' skill at *learning to read* would soon flip-flop to *reading to learn*. When this flip-flop proved to be more of a flop, we knew we needed to intervene or the challenges of our content-rich curriculum would be overwhelming. For nearly a decade we identified and study the best practices we could find and refined them for our classroom. Over time, our reading comprehension instruction progressed and evolved into a four-part approach, which we now call the "Quality Comprehension Model" (Athans & Devine, 2008):

1. Teachers lead *small-group instruction* in *key comprehension strategies* using teacher-selected leveled materials.

2. A *Read-Along Guide*, which is a writing component used by the student, supports the reading instruction.

3. Students take part in *independent activities*, practicing the strategies they've learned through direct instruction or participating in other literacy activities.

4. *Assessments* (formal and informal) that follow each unit of instruction allow teachers to determine if a student has achieved an acceptable level of competency with a skill and also enable students to demonstrate in writing what they have learned.

These practices are largely based on methodologies espoused by authorities such as

Irene Fountas and Gay Su Pinnell (1996, 2001, 2002, 2006), Stephanie Harvey and Anne Goudvis (2000), Ellin Keene (2006), and Ellin Keene and Susan Zimmerman (2007), among others. We've provided some detail on each of these components and invite you to draw comparisons to your own practices.

Small-Group Instruction in Key Comprehension Strategies

Teachers meet with small groups of students who share similar reading skills and abilities. During this instructional time, teachers typically provide direct instruction, model desired outcomes, monitor student progress, and then assign independent work. The process is based on the highly successful "Gradual Release of Responsibility Model," credited largely to David Pearson and Margaret Gallagher (1983).

Key comprehension strategies comprise the content taught during direct instruction. The seventeen strategies we focus on were collected from a variety of sources, as well as some of our own. They represent the skills that good readers use instinctively. Today, most authorities agree that it is best to teach a few strategies so they are learned well (Gambrell, 2007) rather than many that are not learned well. However, we are also aware that many strategies need little or brief direct instruction (Willingham, 2006/2007); and so we balance these ideas, always taking our cues from the direction in which our students' needs point us. Figure 1.1 features brief descriptions of all seventeen strategies.

Figure 1.1. Comprehension Strategies—Skills Good Readers Use

Comprehension Strategies	Description
1. Using Fix-Up Methods When Meaning is Challenged	1. When meaning is lost, students must become aware and take action—reread a passage, review earlier sections, or read on for about two sentences.
2. Finding Word Meaning and Building Vocabulary Using Context Clues	2. Coming across new and unknown words is common. Sounding out, chunking, and linking words are tools to aid us while using context clues to make meaning of words or phrases.
3. Using Visual Text Clues To Figure Out Meaning	3. Text features such as punctuation, type font, spacing, titles, and sub-titles give clues to aid meaning.
4. Making Connections	4. Prior knowledge and experience help us connect to our reading and in turn build our knowledge.
5. Asking Questions	5. Engaged readers ask and answer who, what, when, where, why, and how questions as they read.
6. Visualizing to Support the Text	6. Readers make pictures in their mind of the people, places, or events they're reading about.
7. Making Predictions	7. Engaged readers often make logical predictions about what will happen next in the story.
8. Synthesizing to Gain New Meaning	8. Students construct new meaning to build their knowledge and even create new understandings.
9. Finding Important or Main Idea	9. The important idea is the point or message conveyed in the passage.
10. Identifying Facts and Details	10. These provide substance to a reading passage and support important and main ideas.
11. Telling Fact From Opinion	11. Distinguishing fact from opinion helps readers build a deeper understanding of their reading.

Comprehension Strategies	Description
12. Understanding Sequence	12. Making sense of the order in which ideas are presented enables students to build comprehension.
13. Comparing and Contrasting	13. Considering ways in which ideas relate to something else—either through similarities or differences—is an avenue to develop understanding.
14. Interpreting Figurative Language	14. Understanding creative techniques authors use to convey meaning—such as similes, metaphors, personification, and more—helps aid comprehension.
15. Recognizing Cause-and-Effect Relationships	15. Understanding relationships between ideas helps students grasp meaning by linking outcomes to causes.
16. Drawing Conclusions and Making Inferences	16. Students often use a "sixth sense" or their inferential skills to interpret actions, events, or characters' motives or feelings.
17. Summarizing	17. Providing a brief description of critical information is one way students can hone their comprehension.

From *Quality Comprehension: A Strategic Model of Reading Instruction Using Read-Along Guides, Grades 3–6* by Sandra K. Athans and Denise Ashe Devine. © 2008 International Reading Association. Reprinted with permission.

The Read-Along Guide

The Read-Along Guide is a multipage booklet used by the student during group instruction and/or independent support activities. Figure 1.2 features a selection of reduced-size pages from a Guide. The Guide provides for repeated practice in applying those comprehension strategies that are taught during small group instruction. Likewise, it also provides teachers with a tool to monitor and evaluate student performance. Also featured in the Guide is a reading response section, encouraging students to engage in the reading in a unique, less structured way. The Guides are indisputably one of the most critical components used within this approach.

Figure 1.2. Student Read-Along Guide

_____'s Read-Along Guide

The Courage of Sarah Noble
By Alice Dalgliesh

In this Read-Along Guide, we'll be working on four strategies:

1. **Understanding Sequence**

2. **Recognizing Cause and Effect**

3. **Making Predictions**

4. **Finding Meaning in Context**

1

---

1. **Understanding Sequence** – The order in which things happen in a passage is called sequence. Sometimes clue words such as first, next, last, or others clearly signal an order. Other times, there are no signals and you must carefully retrace actions, steps, or events to check their order. These can be tricky, especially if you are asked to place *multiple* events in correct order. That's because you must always check what came before the event *as well as* what came after it, too. Yikes, that's a lot of information to juggle! As you read your book, you'll be asked to order events around those provided by your teacher.

2. **Recognizing Cause and Effect** – Often events or ideas in a passage are somehow linked together, such as in a cause and effect connection. Here, *what* happens is called the *effect*. Also, *why* it happens is called the *cause*. Sometimes clue words such as since, because, as a result, or others clearly show that connection between what happened and why. Other times, you can easily find cause and effect ideas by asking yourself two questions:
   1. *What* happened? (this will tell you the *effect*)
   2. *Why* did it happen? (this will tell you the *cause*)

As you read your book, you'll be given either a cause or effect found in your book, and then you'll be asked to identify its cause or effect connection.

3. **Making Predictions** – Trying to figure out what will happen next in a story is just plain fun! Finding out if you're right or wrong is often what keeps you interested in a reading passage. Clues certainly come in handy when you're trying to make *good* predictions. Clues can be found in a title or in facts and details in the passage. They can also come from characters' actions or thoughts. Clues can be anywhere!

In the Reader Response section, you'll be making some predictions about the next reading passage.

4. **Finding Meaning in Context** – Let's keep practicing this strategy! Here, we'll even learn some interesting new words that describe things from long ago! As you read your book, you'll be asked to figure out the meaning of words using clues.

2

Pages **Chapter 2 pg. 6-12**
Directions: Let's practice Sequencing Events. Complete the chart.

Sarah and her father knock on the cabin door.
↓
Sarah meets a woman and and asks to stay at her house. She talks to her kids.
↓
Lemuel and Robert teased Sarah about the Indians.
↓
Sarah was going to bed but she felt uncomfortable about Indians.

Pages **Chapter 3 pg. 13-18**
Directions: Let's practice Cause & Effect. Complete the chart.

Cause (why)	Effect (what)
Sarah did not want her father to shoot the deer.	Sarah's father put down his gun.
Sarah said that Thomas should look well.	She put a flower by his ear.

4

Practice using our Word Identification Strategies:

1. "Sound Out" the Word
2. Use Context Clues
3. "Chunk" the Word
4. Link the Word
5. Think About What Makes Sense
6. Look For Smaller Words
7. Other: I knew the word
8. Other: Dictionary

Page #	Difficult Word	Strategy Used	Definition
29	lively	5, 6	full of life
30	mortar	} 2	a tool to grind
30	pestle		things like corn
33	scarlet	2	the color dark red
36	squaw	2	family (wife)
37	mounting	5	get on, put on
37	solemn	2	serious
40	willing	1	eagerly
42	dew	7, 2	condensation
43	wailing	7, 2	a loud yell
44	raided	5	attack
46	tiresome	2	bored or sick of something
47	fretful	1	worrying
50	wigwam	5	an Indian home

16

Independent Reading Activities

Although students are provided with small-group, teacher-led direct instruction in specific comprehension strategies, they also work independently. The type of independent work and/or the length of time allowed for this activity varies among reading groups. It is often based on what occurs during the small group, teacher-led activity. For example, one group might need more support with a teacher, which would then cut into that group's independent work time. Although the teacher's objectives are set before instruction began, adjustments may need to be made based on the monitoring that takes place during the instructional activity.

Assessments

Each unit of instruction, which can last from five to fifteen days, is followed by an assessment. Over time, we've developed two variations of assessments. One is project-based, and the other is patterned after our standardized state assessments and relies on the use of multiple-choice questions as well as short-response and extended-response questions. Although very different in format, the objective of both types of assessments is to determine a student's ability to demonstrate an understanding of reading materials and mastery of the comprehension strategies. A unique assessment follows each unit of instruction, and teachers can decide whether they wish to use a project-based assessment or the more traditional assessment.

Self-Reflection Exercise

You may wish to reflect on your literacy activities to determine if all of the components work together to support your instruction in the best manner possible.

♦ Are there opportunities for students to practice what they've learned?

♦ Is there a way for you to evaluate student understanding on an ongoing basis?

♦ Are there areas that you might wish to consider improving?

Measures of Our Success

We measured the success of this approach in several ways.

♦ *Test Results*—As one measure, we relied on our standardized state test results. Located in a primarily rural area, in the northeastern part of the country, our district comprises a large and economically diverse population in which over 25% of the students, on average, are eligible for free or reduced-price school lunches. Today, the number of students who "pass" our standardized language arts test hovers around 90% in comparison to the 67% who passed when we first began shaping and integrating this model in our classrooms.

♦ *Action Research Results*—We also conducted classroom research over the course of a seven-month period and learned that our students' comprehension increased an average of 23.8% and students' reading performance increased an average of two levels. (Athans, Clarke, Devine, & Sammon, 2005)

♦ *End-Unit Assessments*—Our end-unit assessments provided another avenue for us to analyze. Here we found that students demonstrated an average passing level of skill with nearly all of the comprehension strategies on which they received instruction. Likewise, we learned that students also progressed in their ability to demonstrate in writing their reading comprehension skill.

♦ *Student Participation and Reaction*—Student voices, such as Juanita's, that rang out with excitement about reading is one measure that clearly confirmed we had affected students positively and thoughtfully.

Our Research Findings on Motivation

Although we had good reason to be pleased with our progress, there was other information we had learned from our classroom studies, and it was rather gloomy; namely, that motivation has a major effect on student progress. In an otherwise successful approach, approximately one-fifth of our students were not achieving this same level of success. These were the Caitlyns and the Stevens who, although provided with comparable instruction and equally capable of succeeding, did not benefit like their peers. This was troubling.

Does This Happen in Your Classroom?

I remember looking at the data on the spreadsheets and being confused by the awkward lack of growth that seemed out-of-place for a handful of students. Most of us were puzzled at first. There seemed to be no immediate explanation for these results, especially as our most struggling readers were reaching great heights and even outperforming their more skilled classmates. We began discussing options: Was it feasible to provide additional practice time during the day? Could we locate volunteer tutors for one-on-one support during class instructional time? Did we need to modify our approach even further? We spent some time on these matters before one of the teachers remarked that her student, who was among the handful, rarely completed his reading assignments and often did not practice using the strategies in his Read-Along Guide. From there a pattern began to emerge among the small group of students, and we were able to directly link their effort to their performance. We realized that there was a much more complex problem than we had first imagined and that all of our proposed solutions would most probably have little, if any, positive impact.

Ms. Stietz, Fourth-Grade Teacher

Why Not Modify Our Reading Approach?

Certainly this question came up. All of us were versed in theories and practices that helped us with the daunting task of diversifying our instructional approaches. The pioneering work of Carol Ann Tomlinson (2001) gave us direction in considering a student's readiness, interests, and learning styles. We also worked diligently to incorporate activities, experiences, and even assessments that would cater to students' varying avenues of strength in keeping with the multiple intelligences model espoused by Howard Gardner (1983). It seemed we were already differentiating instruction on many different levels.

- ♦ Differentiating our approach

  - Students were grouped together based on reading level and academic need. (Fountas & Pinnell, 2001)

  - Students were reading leveled texts appropriately matched to their instructional skill level. (Fountas & Pinnell, 2001)

  - Support teachers, working together with the classroom teacher, were free to recommend and modify instruction even further, such as by requesting fewer practice examples in the Read-Along Guide to support instruction and more examples to extend instruction, or by permitting variation in the length of students' responses.

  - Instructional modifications outlined in any student's Individualized Education Program (IEP) were incorporated into the reading approach and were carefully monitored.

- ♦ Varied classroom configurations

  - Incorporated into the instructional approach were a variety of class arrangements—some small group, some independent work, and some paired activities.

- ♦ Flexibility within instruction

  - As students practiced working through the strategies in their Read-Along Guide, there was not one "right" answer (and few, if any, wrong answers), permitting students tremendous flexibility in their individual approach to their reading.

- ♦ Varied literacies

  - The approach also included many forms of literacy: reading, writing, listening, speaking, and thinking. It even included the newer literacies such as visual literacies (Kajder, 2006) and others that reflected the use of new technologies (Karchmer, Mallette, Kara-Soteriou, & Leu, 2005). Our approach was not stymied by routine.

♦ Modifications within the assessments

  • We devised two types of assessments that we often alternated. One was patterned after our state tests, which we referred to as a "traditional assessment." A second was a "project-based assessment" that might include drawing or creating picture books, making a commercial, acting out a play, or other activities. Likewise, even within the more traditional-based assessment, we provided some element of choice, such as by enabling students to select one of two written assignments, for example, a comical news article for a school paper or a persuasive essay.

We had incorporated many unique characteristics that would appeal to a broad and diverse group of students, and we could gracefully finesse them with the same kind of decision-making ease with which one selects an outfit to wear.

Resource Selection

In addition to varying the instruction, the instructional formats, and even the assessments, we were also conscious of the reading resources we selected to use in our instructional units. During the early years of building our approach, we aggressively reviewed resources and materials and scraped together funds to bring the very best books and other literature that we could find to our students. We searched for texts that would align not only with our units in language arts (such as genre and author studies), but also within our social studies and science curricula. We requested review copies of trade books, small-format guided-reading texts, children's magazines, and more, to determine not only if the content was well presented but also if the materials seemed easy-to-use for our strategy-based comprehension approach. We also looked for text features that we hoped would engage the students and provide something beyond what our textbooks, videos, class newspapers, and other more traditional instructional materials included. Even today, we work hard to remain current, seek out new works, and watch for titles that have pizzazz! Our collections are truly exciting.

Self-Reflection Exercise

You may wish to reflect on your own literacy strategies to determine a comfort level with your degree of differentiation, addressing student learning styles, and whether or not you provide choice in your activities.

  ♦ Are your collections contemporary?

  ♦ Even if you are working with a basal series, are you able to supplement with high-interest and content-aligned materials?

Enabling Everyone to Succeed

Generally, we worked very hard to make everyone succeed, and for the most part, everyone did. Rather than altering our approach, we delved into the habits of those students who were not making progress comparable to their peers.

Delving into Our Students' Habits

As a component of our initial classroom research (Athans et al., 2005), we created a number of monitoring and assessing methods. We now took a closer look at some of these devices hoping to determine why our approach wasn't as successful for some students as for others. What we found was a direct correlation between the degree of success students had on the assessments and the degree to which they were prepared and participated during instruction. In all cases, students who were prepared and participated passed the assessments, and those who were not prepared or who did not participate (often the two were linked) did not pass. Likewise, some of the typical notes that appeared on the Student Daily Checklist, a device used to record anecdotal notes, for students who did not pass the assessments brought to light some specific behaviors (Figure 1.3).

Figure 1.3. Behaviors/Performance of Struggling Students

Preparation

♦ Read-Along Guide left at home

♦ Incomplete work

♦ Little detail provided

♦ Examples lack thoughtfulness and depth

♦ Repeated examples teacher provided

♦ Illegible writing; unable to share responses

♦ Page is missing from Read-Along Guide

Participation

♦ Apathetic response to teacher support

♦ Did not contribute to discussions

♦ Was unable to model appropriate response

♦ Unwilling to comment on classmate's journal

♦ Unprepared and unable to participate

♦ Inappropriate response to classmate's examples

♦ Withdrawn from instructional activities

♦ Belligerent response to student aid

♦ Immature reaction to content

♦ Attendance issues—absence from school or arrived late for group instruction

♦ Completed incorrect section of Read-Along Guide

Our findings suggested that these students were disengaged and exhibited behaviors that showed their lack of participation in instruction. This was the major difference that set this group of students apart from their classmates. As a result, we recognized that we might have to work to change student work habits instead of changing our reading approach, especially as we already determined that that our approach proved successful for most students.

A Focus on Motivating Students

Based on this new direction in our studies (Athans, Devine, Henry, Parante, & Sammon, 2006), we investigated numerous methods of motivating *all* students. We desperately wanted to tackle the challenges posed by the Stevens and Caitlyns in our classrooms. Yet, we did not want to neglect the others. As a result, we decided to try to identify ways of motivating all students no matter where a student's starting point was.

Different Approaches

Ask three people their views on student motivation and you'll likely end up with three vastly different perspectives. The same is true of researchers and specialists who study the complex issue of motivation; despite all agreeing it is a critical area of concern, there seems to be as many possible approaches to take as there are specialists studying the issue. Yet, this is a good thing for today's educators who don't necessarily need to find one correct solution to the problem; rather, they can pick and choose solutions that work best in their unique classrooms. There's no need to reinvent the wheel when it needs only to be realigned for a smoother ride. However, what today's educators do need to identify upfront is the problem. What do they want to change? What is the problem?

Figure 1.4 lists some of the works on motivation we reviewed together with statements from each work that characterize the various points of view of the authors of the works. Likewise, insights into students' reading motivation from pioneers such as Guthrie and Wigfield (1977) and Gambrell, Palmer, Codling, and Mazzoni (1996), helped us delve deeper into motivational factors directly linked to reading. We also were aware of disturbing findings, such as those uncovered through the national survey of motivation (Donahue, Daane, & Yin, 2005), indicating that a majority of fourth graders did not view reading as a favorable or enjoyable activity nor did they think that they learned much from reading a book. Certainly, these impacted our approach to motivating all students. In addition to these experts and their research-based findings, there were others who crossed into the motivation arena who specialized in differentiated instruction and multiple intelligence theory, among other areas. Student motivation remains a topic that is addressed from multiple perspectives.

Figure 1.4. Selected Bibliography of Books on Motivation and Differing Views

♦ Blackburn, Barbara R., *Classroom Motivation from A to Z: How to Engage Your Students in Learning*. Larchmont, NY: Eye On Education, 2005.

"Some teachers fall into the same trap. We look for the latest quick fix to help us deal with the ever-increasing challenges we face with today's students....The solution to many of the challenges you face is not purchasing the latest program; it is a focused effort to provide your students an environment in which they can thrive."

♦ Lavoie, Richard, *The Motivation Breakthrough: 6 Secrets to Turning On the Tuned-Out Child*. New York: Touchstone, 2007.

"There are eight basic motivational forces that inspire human beings to action and sustained effort. [The eight motivators include: Gregariousness (the need to fit in), Aggression, Autonomy, Power, Status, Recognition, Inquisitiveness, and Affiliation.] Each of us is inspired to some degree by each of these forces. But the extent to which you are motivated by each of them creates a 'motivation profile' that is unique to you."

♦ Mendler, Allen N., *Motivating Students Who Don't Care: Successful Techniques for Educators*. Bloomington, IN: Solution Tree, 2000.

"Students are missing the idea that it is their responsibility to learn information, practice material, and attend school. They often feel as though they should be adequately entertained. Feeling good has become more valued than working hard."

♦ Rogers, Spence, & the Peak Learning Systems' Team, *Teaching Tips: 105 Ways to Increase Motivation & Learning*. Conifer, CO: Peak Learning Systems, 1999.

"All people, including students, are intrinsically motivated to learn—they just may not be motivated to learn what we have to teach."

♦ Sagor, Richard, *Motivating Students and Teachers in an Era of Standards*. Alexandria, VA: The Association for Supervision and Curriculum Development, 2003.

"Is it inevitable that the pursuit of standards will discourage and frustrate more teachers and students: If so, should society begin to brace itself for a greater number of dropouts and early retirements?"

♦ Stix, Andi, & Frank Hrbek, *Teachers as Classroom Coaches: How to Motivate Students Across the Content Areas*. Alexandria, VA: The Association for Supervision and Curriculum Development, 2006.

"Our approach emphasizes bringing out the talents of our students so that they can perform academic content in front of spectators and teammates. When the content comes alive in this way, students become engaged and motivated."

We could hear many of our concerns and ideal outcomes voiced in the ideas of these specialists. Still, we found we may have agreed more strongly with one specialist than with another. Also, as classroom teachers, we may not have had an option to reject concerns about issues such as standardized testing, issues that we felt obligated to support. (Regardless of our personal views, we agreed with the focus on promoting adequate reading, writing, and thinking skills.) Clearly, there were numerous paths for us to take. It became evident that another critical step to take in creating our motivation improvement initiative was to reflect on what matters most—and we thought two ideas mattered most:

1. What goals had we set for our students in terms of our reading approach?

2. How did motivation (or lack of it) play a role in preventing our students from achieving those goals? What behaviors were demonstrated?

The two ideas seemed linked and at the very core of the approaches that the specialists were addressing.

Creating a Vision and Setting Goals for Our Motivation Improvement Initiative

Most of us believed we could clearly articulate our goals for our students, especially as we had focused our efforts on our reading approach. Specifically, we wanted our students to engage in our successful reading approach by

♦ participating in small-group instruction;

♦ completing their strategy practice in their Read-Along Guides; and

♦ demonstrating use of the comprehension strategies and what they had learned during instruction within the end-unit assessments.

For those who were already meeting these requirements, we wanted them to

♦ use their best effort consistently; and

♦ demonstrate autonomy in building their reading skill.

Basically, we wanted our students to perform academically within a framework that supported growth in literacy. This was the dominant goal that all of the other behavioral goals supported.

Likewise, we realized that we had our own views that demonstrated how we would motivate students toward those goals. Although, at first, this may have been an unspoken philosophy that was supported (perhaps unknowingly) through our actions, we soon recognized that this, too, needed to be articulated: *We wanted students to be held accountable for these goals, which we believed were both reasonable and attainable.*

Although there were numerous circumstances that would challenge this philosophy, we maintained our conviction that all students would be held to these same goals, and we would help clear the path for those who needed it.

In addition to reviewing our personal feelings about motivation, we also were quick to identify colleagues whose opinions we didn't completely share. Although we would return to this differing of opinions as we developed our plan, it was useful to define our goals in terms of what we wanted as well as what we didn't want.

A Peek into the Classroom

Ms. Martin and Mr. Brown really liked coteaching with each other, but they had very different views about their expectations for student performance. Ms. Martin was responsible for assisting four of Mr. Brown's students who struggled with reading. Although they worked with some of the same instructional materials, Ms. Martin modified her students' assignments and because of this, often pulled the students aside for instruction. When she graded the students' work and returned it to Mr. Brown, two issues became clear: Not only did her grades appear to be inflated when compared to Mr. Brown's, but her comments on the students' work reflected more praise than he would have given for the same quality of work. They would have to reach a better, more mutual understanding on these matters and got together briefly to review and align their efforts to assist the students. They discussed their different grading styles and agreed that Ms. Martin would support the students' good effort through verbal praise and a sticker chart. She also agreed to help her students set goals to raise their expectations.

Keeping an ongoing dialogue with all colleagues who are collaborating with you, as shown in the vignette above, may be the best course of action to take when your opinions differ.

Had we not paused for this self-reflective exercise, we would not have had such a clearly defined direction. It seemed we had created a philosophy statement that aligned with our starting point and drove our initiative.

Your Motivation Improvement Action Plan

The Motivation Improvement Action Plan is a step-by-step plan you can devise to meet your own classroom needs. A black line master appears in Appendix B (page 149). Using the Motivation Tips that follow here and in subsequent chapters, you can easily develop your plan by adding ideas and strategies as you encounter them in your reading. This plan best represents the hands-on approach we use in our workshops and in our grade-level meetings when we were first trying to effect positive change in student motivation. A sample plan is also featured showing how the tips might be applied and tailored by a classroom teacher.

Motivation Improvement Initiative Tip #1: Determine a Starting Point for Your Motivation Improvement Initiative

Selecting a starting point to guide your effort is critical. Without a broad starting point, your motivation problem may never be considered a truly solvable problem; instead, it may remain a solutionless burden to bear. It's not only very possible that this starting point may change; it is highly likely that it will. Nonetheless, it is a beginning. We began by focusing on our language arts instruction, specifically reading.

Is there an area you've already identified as needing improvement? Are students struggling to comprehend nonfiction passages? Is the figurative language in fables and poetry proving too challenging for many of your students to grasp? Focusing on a specific genre may be a good beginning. Many educators who work with lower and mid elementary students may be responsible for providing instruction in all subjects. As such, they might have several considerations when trying to determine a starting point. Is there an element of literacy instruction within a content area such as science or social studies that needs the most immediate attention? For example, fifth-grade students may be required to prepare a written report to include with a science fair project. If such a report has proven troublesome for students, could it become the starting point for your motivation improvement initiative? Your focus might also be targeted at a specific project in an instructional unit, for example a focus on a particular writing assignment, such as a research paper, that falls within your writing curriculum.

Perhaps the starting point is a school district initiative, such as ways of improving poor performance on a state test. Here, a team of teachers could be selected to participate in the motivation improvement quest and be asked to contribute to the effort through their participation in a predetermined manner or in a manner they collaboratively devise.

Our experience suggests that jotting down your starting point is useful for several reasons. It not only makes it a concrete issue (lest you need reminders), but more importantly, it provides the impetus to suggest that hope will come in the form of a solution, something that is perhaps long overdue. Lastly, it is a starting point that is sure to change over time, as successes are met and new challenges are encountered. It will become a traceable process that will serve as a reminder for future solutions to future challenges.

Some Examples of Starting Points

We initially decided to link our motivation improvement efforts to our general language arts reading approach. Here are others that we have gathered from workshops and discussions with other educators:

♦ Language-based issues across the curriculum for schools with high English Language Learner (ELL) populations.

♦ Literacy instruction within all content areas (social studies, science, etc.), particularly at the upper elementary grade levels, where students' motivational issues further complicate the challenges of a rigorous curriculum.

♦ Methods of assisting students in literacy-based activities who receive self-contained, specialized resource instruction. In these small classes every student struggles, which is a unique set of circumstance that larger, randomly grouped classrooms do not typically encounter.

♦ Methods of addressing students' literacy needs when family matters are so tumultuous that they interfere with a student's ability to perform academically.

♦ Ways to help those students whose literacy skills haven't been met over time and have spiraled out of control, creating a perpetual cycle of failure.

As Figure 1.5 (page 20) shows, this teacher has selected as a starting point a specific writing assignment that is required in her third quarter marking period—a research paper on a U.S. president. She has also added a larger scope to her starting point—to improve student writing.

Motivation Improvement Initiative Tip #2: Define Your Goals By Reviewing Your Concerns

One way to set goals in a motivation improvement initiative is to first review your concerns. *What's on Your Plate* is a well-known technique we've used in our workshops to help others pinpoint areas of concern. Through the use of this playful idiom, we ask everyone to list what they believe is *on their plate* in terms of their students' motivation (they actually list these concerns on a paper plate). This allows everyone to consider their unique challenges, no matter how general or specific they might be, as a starting point upon which to set goals. Figure 1.6 (page 21) provides some examples of concerns and barriers teachers may believe are "on their plate" regarding student motivation.

From the selection on their plate, participants then "cluster" like ideas and prioritize them. The refined list becomes their specific goals. Figure 1.6 demonstrates this process for the teacher championing the research paper project. Figure 1.7 (page 22) is the sample plan that now features the goals from Tip #2.

In addition to launching a goal-setting process, this exercise also helps participants realize that many of these issues are global. They are not a reflection of any one individual's instruction, classroom management practices, or overall classroom performance. Realizing this, individuals may feel less prone to working in isolation to fix their problems.

What also may become evident is whether or not you may wish to collaborate with others to create your motivation improvement plan. Certainly it's okay to begin small, such as with one individual setting classroom goals, but it's also okay to consider that the plan may grow larger and require support. Collaboration may become critical and working with others to address challenges may be key for the successful implementation of your plan. This initial exercise is a fine beginning to set goals and also to consider possible motivational activities. If areas become clear for collaboration, you may wish to note these in your plan (as shown in the sample in Figure 1.7, page 22).

(Text continues on page 23.)

Figure 1.5. The Motivation Improvement
Action Plan Sample with Tip #1

Page 1 of 2

Starting Point: *Improve student performance on third-quarter Presidential Research Paper (and explore overall improvement in writing)*

Goals:

- _____
- _____
- _____

Collaborators: _____

_____

Philosophy Statement: _____

_____

_____

_____

Expression of the Ideal: _____

_____

Superhero Strategies:

1. _____

   Ways to Adapt: _____

   _____

   _____

   _____

   Collaborators: _____

   _____

2. _____

   Ways to Adapt: _____

   _____

   _____

   _____

   Collaborators: _____

   _____

Figure 1.6. "What's On Your Plate" Activity to Generate Goals

On My Plate

1. Students aren't applying their research skills
(even when skills are practiced and reseources are provided)
2. Little attention is placed on grammar, punctuation, and spelling
3. Organization of ideas is weak
4. Writing process seems complicated by students'
lack of content knowledge on the topic (i.e., specific presidents)
5. Not enough effort put into reading and understanding biographies
6. Interruptions throughout Language Arts instructional time
7. More support for some students is needed

Clusters

a) Issues in #2, 3, 4, and 7 involve the writing process
b) Issues in #1, 5, and 7 involve the research process
c) Issue in #6 involves broader school functions

Figure 1.7. The Motivation Improvement
Action Plan Sample with Tip #2

Starting Point: _Improve student performance on third-quarter Presidential Research Paper (and explore overall improvement in writing)_

Goals:
- _Students to apply their beginning research skills (learned and practiced)_
- _Improve writing skills and writing process skills_
- _Produce a quality research paper that demonstrates use of writing process and beginning research skills_

Collaborators: _Librarian and Writing Support Instructor_

Philosophy Statement: _____
_____
_____
_____

Expression of the Ideal: _____
_____

Superhero Strategies:
1. _____
   Ways to Adapt: _____
   _____
   _____
   _____

   Collaborators: _____
   _____

2. _____
   Ways to Adapt: _____
   _____
   _____
   _____

   Collaborators: _____
   _____

Motivation Improvement Initiative Tip #3:
Set the Tone—Establish a Philosophy Statement

Articulating your philosophy on motivation and clarifying the angle you wish to take may become necessary. This is especially true if your initiative requires that you work collaboratively with other educators.

To begin, you might want to review Figure 1.4 (page 15), which capsulizes points of view of several well-known motivation experts. Determine your comfort level with these statements to initiate your soul-searching about your philosophy. Why do the various views affect you as they do? Answers to this question should unveil some of your beliefs.

Some other questions to consider that might help you recognize your views are:

♦ What are your hopes for your students?

♦ What barriers do you see getting in the way of these hopes?

♦ What are required expectations for your students?

♦ What barriers do you see getting in the way of their success at meeting these expectations?

By considering responses to these questions, you might find you're juggling between hopes and expectations, and likewise that you're determining your empathetic reaction to issues that need consideration as you develop your plan.

Lastly, it's always helpful to consider others' perspectives. Don't hesitate to speak to colleagues or even to review a mission statement that your district has prepared. Considering your reaction to the outcome may help you better identify your own views.

Figure 1.8 (page 24) features the sample Motivation Improvement Plan that includes a philosophy statement for Tip #3. As shown, the teacher's note, "each according to his/her need," the issue of student capability (mentioned earlier in this chapter) was discussed as the teacher prepared her statement. Having placed this statement in the plan ensures that all collaborators will monitor and review this throughout the improvement process.

Figure 1.8. The Motivation Improvement
Action Plan Sample with Tip #3

Starting Point: _Improve student performance on third-quarter Presidential Research Paper_
(and explore overall improvement in writing)

Goals:
- _Students to apply their beginning research skills (learned and practiced)_
- _Improve writing skills and writing process skills_
- _Produce a quality research paper that demonstrates use of writing process and_
  beginning research skills

Collaborators: _Librarian and Writing Support Instructor_

Philosophy Statement: _All students will be held accountable for demonstrating use of all_
skills and strategies which were taught and practiced for writing a research paper
(Each according to his/her ability)

Expression of the Ideal: _Meet with success and develop a belief in the importance of the_
skill and come to value the process involved.

Superhero Strategies:

1. _____

   Ways to Adapt: _____

   _____

   _____

   _____

   Collaborators: _____

   _____

2. _____

   Ways to Adapt: _____

   _____

   _____

   _____

   Collaborators: _____

   _____

How Would You Motivate These Students?

Case Study #1: Mina

The students who had been seated together with Mina voted her to be their discussion leader for a new activity; they agreed she had a take-charge attitude, knew all sorts of information (and wasn't shy about sharing it), and was friendly and helpful in the classroom. Mina was happy with her job assignment, confident that she would do well. But she grew mildly uneasy as Mr. Carl explained that the discussion leader would begin by sharing his or her response to yesterday's independent reading assignment (which was occasionally completed as homework) with the group. Although Mina could quickly pick up information, she rarely spent much time on homework and typically looked for shortcuts whenever possible. She was satisfied just getting by with what she figured Mr. Carl would find "acceptable." In her new role as discussion leader, Mina opened her journal and began reading her short response. She had completed both the reading (which she skimmed) and her written response during yesterday's class time, and was now struggling to figure out her scribbled words; she couldn't read her writing. (See Appendix A, page 143, for an outcome of Case Study #1: Mina.)

Case Study #2: Kirk

Kirk was unpredictable. At times, he'd be totally prepared for class and would participate in activities and provide thoughtful ideas. Other times, he'd rummage through his backpack looking for his materials, disturbing those near him with dramatic sighs and groans. He was often removed from the classroom when he behaved this way, and ended up working under the principal's watchful eye for an hour or two. Similarly, he might one day happily announce that he'd completed all of his work and hold up an assignment as if for inspection, while at other times, he'd claim he lost his work or didn't complete it because of a variety of unlucky circumstances that tripped him up. These troubles had not escaped the attention of many of Kirk's teachers who had tried to work with him year after year. Kirk's parents were also well aware of his school difficulties and were unsure how to help him. (See Appendix A, page 143, for an outcome of Case Study #2: Kirk.)

Case Study #3: Jennifer

Jennifer often complained that she was hungry as I would start my lesson. It was distracting for the other students who immediately chimed in with questions: "Why didn't you buy breakfast this morning?" or "Why don't you eat breakfast at home?" Ten to fifteen minutes would pass before we could get back on track, and I could start the lesson the classroom teacher and I had prepared. Rarely was I able to complete everything I needed to. I wanted Jennifer to participate in our class discussions and instruction, and I had every intention of holding her accountable for her learning as I did the other students, but I was also bothered by the fact that she had nothing to eat that morning. Admittedly, I was torn between feeling sorry for her and wanting her to focus on instruction so she could stay on schedule with her classroom teacher's expectations as well as my own expectations. Still, on the days she was hungry, this wasn't going to happen, and I knew it would cause some friction between her classroom teacher and me. (See Appendix A, page 144, for an outcome of Case Study #3: Jennifer.)

2

Superhero
Strategies to the Rescue!

Superhero Strategies can be integrated into your instructional processes. Virtual shape-shifters, they can blend and fit in with many existing literacy-based activities. They provide novelty and variety, while also emphasizing what matters most—literacy improvement!

We've learned from some of our most successful practices in education that creating a *process* within which to make improvements presents us with a good systematic plan that, once learned, can be used repeatedly. For example, using the writing process with its various stages of prewriting, drafting, editing, and rewriting provides students with a systematic method of tackling a variety of writing assignments. Likewise, the scientific method with its steps of testing a hypothesis, collecting and reviewing data, and drawing conclusions also provides a systematic process for uncovering answers to a plethora of questions. Like these processes, creating one to support your motivation improvement initiative may impact its chance of success; it may actually present us with our *best chance* of affecting positive change in student behaviors. Creating a vision and determining a starting point, discussed in Chapter 1, are the initiating steps in this process. The next step is to add some novelty and variety to existing instructional activities and procedures. Systematically giving kids multiple opportunities to succeed and showing them how this can be achieved within classroom routine is key.

Motivation Improvement—Process Strategies

Giving students ample opportunity to demonstrate improvement and to share in the rewards of the improvement initiative are important. The former supports the need of getting them to "buy into" or accept the idea, while the latter recognizes them for their accomplishments. The following techniques address both concepts and can, with some work, become routine within your classroom instruction. Also, they are flexible and may be integrated into your daily language arts activities or reserved to be used with some consistency in a specified activity, such as during your small-reading-group instruction. You can choose when and where to use them. Although some techniques are unique, others are based on general practices touted by many of the motivational specialists mentioned in Chapter 1. In this chapter, they have been reshaped to align with the activities and objectives of typical literacy-based instruction.

In addition to describing the techniques and providing glimpses of what they may "look like" through classroom vignettes, we've included easy-to-use methods for monitoring and evaluating student success in each of them. The reason for this is twofold. First, you'll be able to substantiate student progress and use the information to monitor and adjust your plans. Second, having methods in place that clearly show students how they're performing in relation to expected outcomes could encourage them to assume more responsibility for the choices they make about their actions and behaviors. Monitoring and evaluating these practices also sends a clear message to students that you believe such practices matter and are important. Additionally, we share some of our troubleshooting methods, which we call "Solutions to Keep in Mind," that could prove helpful when you encounter difficulties that temporarily interfere with your success.

The chapter ends with a brief discussion highlighting the few commonalities among all of the strategies. That these highlights are shared among many, if not all, of the strategies, suggests their importance as critical motivation-building factors and thus may strongly influence your degree of success.

Teaming Competitions

The idea of developing a motivationally charged environment by reshaping academic activities so they parallel athletic competitions is one that probably wouldn't take much convincing to support. Most would agree that the rallying support of fans and spectators, not to mention the friendly competition that exists between teammates, has motivated athletes from as early as the ancient Olympic games to today's local high school football rivalries. Also, who among us hasn't witnessed the complete change of attitude and momentum in a student who, although uninspired to write a single-paragraph response to a reading assignment, would risk bruised knees and elbows to slide home when the score was tied at the bottom of the ninth inning and two runners already out?

Bringing the team competition idea into the classroom is one that authorities such as Sagor (2003) and Slaven (1994) enthusiastically support and identify as "cooperative team-learning" strategies. The underlying objective supporting the use of these types of strategies is that the success of the team results from the collective contributions of each individual's *best effort*. Rewarding students based on their best effort as compared to an academic standard of success is one that supports all students no matter how vast the range of skills may be in any given classroom. To most students, this seems fair. Additionally, the benefits of using team strategies are many; those students who may be more skilled in certain areas are inherently encouraged to assist those who may be challenged in those areas. Also, the social structures of the team strategies could spotlight unique social or intrapersonal strengths of some students who may not have received recognition or praise for them in the past. Just as team-learning strategies encourage students to engage in academic activities in playful, fair, and creative team competitions, so, too, has the classroom teacher's role taken on a new twist—one of a "coach," an idea suggested by Stix and Hrbek (2006, p. 11), among others: "The classroom is the playing field, the students are the team, and the teacher, as the coach, holds everything together."

Our intent in introducing some team-competition strategies into our literacy instruction, specifically within our small-group reading activities, was to encourage the peer support and sense of community that we found developed among members of our small, five- to seven-member homogeneous groups. Each member of the group was already connected in that they shared ideas and opinions about the book their group was reading. We wanted to encourage this peer support beyond topics contained in the book. For example, we wondered to what degree individual group members would offer helpful suggestions, provide a watchful buddy-support network, and give guidance to other team members in terms of friendly sharing of successful habits, strategies, or approaches. Although our reading groups were usually homogeneous, in so far as students were reading at similar levels or within a narrow range such as N to P (Fountas & Pinnell, 1996, guided-reading levels distinguishing end of third-grade, early fourth-grade readers), there were still many other factors that often made them seem as if they were heterogeneous. For example, some students may have been very skilled at applying specific comprehension strategies, such as inferencing or interpreting figurative language, whereas others had much difficulty grasping even the meaning of the strategy. Also, some students were very skilled at expressing their ideas verbally as well as in writing (which was evident through their work in their Read-Along Guide, discussed in Chapter 1), while other students had trouble articulating their thoughts in any manner. We hoped that our team competitions would encourage a camaraderie in which an individual's unique strengths would be shared among all members and would, in turn, collectively shore up any given member's specific weakness. This concept seemed very feasible.

As we had previously targeted areas within our literacy-based activities we felt were critical for success, we decided to use these areas as our starting point. As discussed in Chapter 1, whether or not students were *prepared* for their small-group meeting and whether or not they *participated* during that instruction seemed to greatly influence their degree of success. We introduced the idea of having a friendly and fair team competition among the three reading groups, all of which met daily, using these two targeted areas as the criteria for the challenge. Unsurprisingly, the idea was a big hit. Next, we discussed the criteria in more detail. It was important that there be a common understanding of what being prepared for small group instruction and participation during instruction meant. Although both standards had been in place for some time, awarding points to individuals based on how well each met these standards now seemed to breathe new life into what were worn-out expectations of student behavior. Figure 2.1 illustrates the ideas that were brainstormed during this whole-class lesson. Then, in our small groups, we also identified barriers that might prevent some members from meeting those challenges and, more importantly, suggested ways to overcome them. What we ended up with in each group was (a) a network of multiple two- or three-student clusters in which a host of unique strengths were matched to an equally diverse collection of weaknesses; (b) a cheerleader/mascot who clearly had good collaborative interpersonal skills; and (c) an acknowledgement that each individual would have to make independent choices that would contribute to the team's success. Figure 2.2 shows the outcomes from one group discussion.

Figure 2.1. Student Generated Ideas: What it Means to be "Prepared" and to "Participate"

What does it mean to...

Be prepared

- ◆ Finish assignments (your reading and your work in your Read-Along Guide).
- ◆ When your group meets, have a sharpened pencil, your Read-Along Guide, your folder, book, and an eraser.
- ◆ Keep your desk and materials organized so you can arrive at your reading group promptly.
- ◆ Don't forget your glasses, tissues, or other things *you* need.

Participate

♦ Pay attention and listen to whomever is speaking.

♦ Make eye contact with the people you're speaking to.

♦ Focus on what you're doing.

♦ Don't be disrespectful while others are speaking (don't move around in your chair, don't play with erasers and other materials, try not to get distracted).

♦ Respect the teacher and classmates.

♦ Share your ideas correctly.

♦ Add to your Read-Along Guide when you learn ways to improve your ideas.

Figure 2.2. Outcome of Small-Group Discussions: Strengths Noted and Buddy Clusters Established

Group 1:

Nathan—Good understanding of the Revolutionary War. See him if you're unsure about content.

Jamile—Finishes early. Gives clear responses. See him to check the thoroughness of an idea.

Sean—Multitasker. See him to double check that you're prepared and/or if you missed instruction because of music, illness, etc.

Jay—Word wise. See him to double check understanding of vocabulary.

Eric—Good written organization.

Buddy Partners:

Jamile & Nathan & Jay—Help one another complete all tasks & watch pacing.

Sean & Eric—Help one another organize Read-Along Guide entry.

Sean—Cheerleader—Rally group members & check "prepared" status.

Note: Once students get the idea that they are part of a team, they are more open to discussing areas that challenge them (and those of their team members). However, these challenges are not recorded. Instead, each individual's strength is recognized and recorded and "buddy clusters," which are devised to overcome challenges, are also noted. For example, Nathan was greatly challenged by his inability to complete work in a timely manner, which was not noted. However, his strength was that he had a good grasp of the content of the instructional unit, which was noted. He is clustered with two students who can support him with his challenge of completing his work on time. Strategically shaping these introductory discussions so to encourage students to share in a plan that promotes their strengths and shores up their challenges, generates team-building skills, and enthusiasm for team success.

To devise a point system to award teams for their performance, it was important to begin with our basic performance indicators: Were students prepared? Did students participate? However, we soon realized that to make this strategy fair and effective we needed to introduce other parameters that would enable the successful students to challenge themselves and extend their skill while also enabling weaker students to significantly contribute to the team's success. This was done by awarding points if members demonstrated evidence of *troubleshooting* solutions to problems they encountered, and if students *challenged* themselves to extend their performance. Likewise, from an idea adopted from Sagor (2003), we awarded points based on gains made to each member's progress on our end-unit formal assessments. Our point value system was presented to students as follows:

- *Prepared*—each participant awarded 1 point

- *Participation*—each participant awarded 1 point

- *Trouble Shooting Success (TSS)*—teams awarded 1 point for each TSS

- *Challenges (C)*—teams awarded ½ point for each challenge

- *End-Unit Assessment*—each participant awarded a point value equal to the growth (or decline) in their end-unit assessment

All points were then averaged by the number of members in each team. Point values for the first four categories were collected, posted, and averaged daily. The end-unit assessment was tabulated only at the end of a unit (each unit lasted from 5 to 15 days); however, it held the greatest potential for significantly altering the outcome of the team competition. We believed this system encouraged team cooperation and peer assistance and was fair to all participants.

A Peek into the Classroom

Prior to starting the "friendly" competitions, Ms. Bell was concerned about those students who had a variety of problems: keeping up with the workload, understanding the content they read, using good effort, even behavioral issues. Would they be open to accepting help from their peers? Would help given within the context of a fun-filled team competition prove more effective than her previous efforts? Would other team members accept the challenging graciously? Ms. Bell knew she'd be asking a lot of everybody, but soon she was relieved to see that small clusters of students who had paired themselves together were making progress with some of these trouble areas. Crystal seemed to flourish with Juli-anne's helpful guidance, and William's behavior improved as he seemed more comfortable seeking help from Justine when he didn't understand the directions or the reading passage his group had been assigned. Although this didn't happen in every case, it happened often enough to support the continued use of these friendly competitions. Students remained interested and enthusiastic and most felt successful.

Methods for Monitoring

Figure 2.3 represents a version of our Student Daily Checklist Form (see Figure 1.3, page 13) modified for use with the Teaming Competitions. Many of the teachers already had this monitoring device in place during their small-group instruction. Adding space for recording student strengths and buddy clusters, as well as a tally system to re-

Figure 2.3. Student Daily Checklist
Modified for Teaming Competitions

Student Daily Checklist

Instructional Unit: _Revolutionary War_

Group 1 (strengths & buddy clusters): _____   Daily Tally: _____

Nathan	Good understanding of the Revolutionary War. See him if you're unsure about content.
Jamile	Finishes early. Gives clear responses. See him to check the thoroughness of an idea.
Sean	Multi-tasker. See him to double check that you're prepared or if you missed instruction due to music, illness, etc.
Jay	Word wise. See him to double check understanding of vocabulary.
Eric	Good written organization

Buddy Partners:

Jamile & Nathan & Jay — Help one another complete all tasks & watch pacing

Sean & Eric — Help one another organize Read-Along Guide entry

Sean — Cheerleader – Rally group members & check 'prepared' status

Date	Total	Average
4/15	8/5	1.6
4/16	10/5	2

Name _____ Nathan _____
4/15 (1) prepared   (1) participation
Nice Job!
4/16 (1) prepared   (1) participation
Great!
_____ () prepared   () participation
_____ () prepared   () participation
_____ () prepared   () participation
_____ () prepared   () participation

Name _____ Jamile _____
4/15 (1) prepared   (.5) participation
Let's work on group discussion skills
4/16 (1) prepared   (1) participation
Much improved, Jamile. Great!
_____ () prepared   () participation
_____ () prepared   () participation
_____ () prepared   () participation
_____ () prepared   () participation

Name _____ Sean _____
4/15 (1) prepared   (1) participation
Nice
4/16 (1) prepared   (1) participation
Good work rallying team!
_____ () prepared   () participation
_____ () prepared   () participation
_____ () prepared   () participation
_____ () prepared   () participation

Name _____ Jay _____
4/15 (.5) prepared   (1) participation
Missing support. Watch details, Jay
4/16 (1) prepared   (1) participation
Good improvement.
_____ () prepared   () participation
_____ () prepared   () participation
_____ () prepared   () participation
_____ () prepared   () participation

Name _____ Eric _____
4/15 (1) prepared   (0) participation
Eric, let's discuss how we can help.
4/16 (1) prepared   (1) participation
Bravo, Eric! Stellar Improvement!
_____ () prepared   () participation
_____ () prepared   () participation
_____ () prepared   () participation
_____ () prepared   () participation

Name _____
_____ () prepared   () participation
_____ () prepared   () participation
_____ () prepared   () participation
_____ () prepared   () participation
_____ () prepared   () participation
_____ () prepared   () participation

cord a number of points awarded for daily activities, was simple. Likewise, most teachers already had a system in place to record student progress on an end-unit assessment that was equally effective for tracking students' progress over time, which was needed for the final area in teaming competitions. Consequently, no additional review of a student's assessment was needed. This information can be transferred to a form that could be easily retrievable and that is stored with the other materials used during small-group instruction.

Solutions to Keep in Mind

♦ *Frequency*—The Teaming Competitions present a flexible approach that teachers may use in many different ways. Some teachers might choose to use them with challenging units such as content-rich units that align with the social studies or science curriculum. A unit on poetry might also be a good choice as some students struggle to grasp elements of this genre. When and how often to use this approach is a decision best left to the teacher.

♦ *Keep the competition friendly*—As we all know, students have their own comfort level with competitive events; some are extremely competitive and assertive, whereas others are less so. At the start of these events, or perhaps as new averaged scores are posted, some students may become overly zealous about the competition. This could affect their sense of fair play and their willingness to help teammates. Reminding students about their unique contribution to the team's success, as well as discussing their responsibility of making independent choices that will support the team, may need some reinforcing. As mentioned earlier, the teacher's role as "coach" to realign, direct, and encourage members to rally the team with an appropriate sense of fair play and sportsmanship may be called upon.

♦ *Adjustments may be needed to promote a sense of fairness*—Although you make every attempt to make your point system fair, one that provides equity and supports all students who work hard, you might need to make adjustments. Some teachers have resolved matters of fairness by awarding bonus points to students who have perfect end-unit assessment scores, by offering earn-back points if a student is not given points but remedies the situation in a manner the teacher finds acceptable, by offering kindness points if students are in need of coaching on team-building skills, and in other ways that will improve the effectiveness of the team competitions.

♦ *Some individuals may need extra support to keep up*—Although the team competitions will likely engage most students, it may be necessary to help some students who are unable to benefit from the systems already in place. The student support clusters, the cheerleader's rally, and all other infrastructures that have been designed to help students succeed might not reach everyone. It may be necessary to develop an independent support plan with some students. Calling upon the assistance from a parent, holding a special study session prior to an end-unit assessment, or soliciting the help from an outside volunteer or a mentor from another class might help with this type of situation.

A Peek into the Classroom

Donna had a great deal of trouble understanding the ideas in the historical fiction book that her group had been assigned. Although the book aligned with her independent reading level, it presented some content information that was challenging. She had little background knowledge on the Revolutionary War (despite having recently learned about it in her social studies class) and also had a sketchy understanding of the struggles of the slaves during this period in history. Ms. Fletcher determined that Donna would benefit from spending some extra time reading and discussing the book with an adult volunteer who occasionally helped out in her classroom. She spoke to Donna and Donna's mother about the idea and arranged for the volunteer to spend some time before or after school over the course of three days to read, reread, and discuss the concepts in the book. Also, Ms. Fletcher invited Donna and other interested students to a special study session during recess which she held just prior to the end-unit assessment. With this extra support, Donna not only participated more fully during instruction, but she also performed well on her assessment.

♦ *This may not be the right approach for some students*—Some students may suffer so severely from low self-esteem that any type of competitive event that surrounds their academics is stressful. Similarly, some students just don't perform well when competing with their peers. Working with these students independently (discussed above) may help to alleviate these issues. However, it might also be necessary to find another way for these students to participate in the group. They could be "Supply Captains," making sure their team has sticky notes, erasers, and other materials. "Runners" could help teammates collect their materials. You might need to consider alternatives like these. However, you might also find that students gain confidence working in the team format. Careful monitoring may be necessary.

♦ *Rewards*—Teachers may choose to reward students in ways they feel are appropriate. Some teachers may designate certain prizes for the highest-scoring team and other prizes for those that came in second and third. Others may provide recognition awards instead of prizes by featuring student names on a display in the classroom and distributing certificates of accomplishment to the winning team. Another variation on this is using a "totem pole" technique in which the high-scoring group is placed on top of the pole. Selecting rewards that align with your views and philosophy is important, and our intent in providing a varied selection is not to promote one method over another, but instead to offer a range of suggestions.

♦ *Another idea*—Smaller components within a whole-unit instructional activity will work no matter if the groups are heterogeneous or homogeneous.

For example, while preparing for assessments such as spelling or vocabulary tests, teachers could create minicompetitions in which the elements of the team competitions are much smaller and are used only for a brief period of time. Modifications to the point system will need to be made.

Wrap-up on Teaming Competitions

With a little ingenuity, teaming competitions can be integrated into many small-group activities that you already have in place. Adding this twist to your instructional activities builds team skills just as readily as it builds academic skills. Other benefits include piquing the interest and involvement of students who, although shy as independent risk-takers, may be more willing to accept competitive team challenges. Additionally, students who may not normally have the chance to win big, are the ones who can greatly contribute to the team's success.

Integrated Ways to Boost Reading

Literacy research is quick to remind us that children who read are generally better readers than those who don't read. When students have ample opportunity to practice their reading strategies, they move closer to mastering them and to using them automatically while reading. Although some students may have difficulty with this process because of learning or developmental issues, generally the path to successful reading involves reading, reading, and then reading some more. In as much as we all know this to be true, we are also aware that the reverse holds just as much merit; those who don't read, don't often meet with the same degree of success as those who do. Determining how to get the reluctant reader to read, to enjoy reading, and to consider reading a worthwhile activity is a problem that often perplexes many of us. *Literacy Bins* and *Mini Book Club Reading Groups* are activities that are designed to spark interest in reading in reluctant readers and to ignite further participation by all readers. Their objective is to boost reading!

Literacy Bins

Based on the popular literacy stations introduced by Debra Diller (2005), a Literacy Bin is multiunit compartment that houses literary-based activities. Figure 2.4 shows a Literacy Bin where students are selecting activities to complete. Features of the Literacy Bin activities include the following:

- They are designed to boost literacy skills through some combination of reading, writing, thinking, listening, and/or speaking.

- They are aligned thematically to the literacy instruction taking place simultaneously in the classroom.

- They are designed to supplement classroom instruction.

- They address the unique abilities and needs of middle-grade learners.

- They may be completed in combinations of teams and/or independently.

Figure 2.4. Students Selecting Activities from a Literacy Bin

Students can select activities using a variety of methods. For example, teachers might wish to use the popular nine-square tic-tac-toe board where students work toward completing three activities in a horizontal, vertical, or diagonal row. Small prizes can be awarded for the completion of a row or row(s). Figure 2.5 shows a tic-tac-toe board from an instructional unit on Colonial Times, which can be used in this manner. Another method is to create a menu that designates activities as an appetizer, entrée, side dish, or dessert and assigns a point value (Figure 2.6). Students select from the menu options and accumulate points based on their selection. Any type of point-based reward system can be put in place, such as earning a homework pass, computer time, or some other reward. Popular games, menus, treasure maps, and other devices can be used to create a system for selecting activities.

Figure 2.5. A Tic-Tac-Toe Board for an Instructional Unit on Colonial Times

Name _____   Colonial Times   Tic-Tac-Toe

Word Search Colonial Times	It Happened When?	Genius TV Talk Show!
Find and highlight all of the words from the word bank. Get ready to travel back in time!	**Time Line Activity** Can you organize these important events into the correct chronological order? Use the dates as your guide. Look at the sequence of events that unfolds.	A scholarly showing of smarts (Library Pass Needed for Filming) Our extremely intelligent student scholars will share their "smarts" about common questions on the Colonial Period—live—on the popular talk show—*"Genius TV."* They've got smarts, they've got style...and just listen to them speak!
Colonial Leaders Hall of Fame!	**READ** *Read At Home!*	**What Happened… And Why? Cause & Effect!**
Create a portrait of a leader to hang in the Colonial Hall of Fame and include a paragraph about your leader's accomplishments. Select from: Henry Hudson, Peter Minuit, Peter Stuyvesant, John Peter Zenger, Elias Neau, Samuel Fraunces, General George Washington, Joseph Brant, Saguyewatha, and George Clinton.	Have your parent sign your reading list of a minimum of five Colonial nonfiction books. *My Prairie Year* and *Sarah Plain and Tall* are works of historical fiction. You can swap either of these in place of *two* nonfiction titles.	Use a cause & effect chart and find at least five examples in the book *New York as a Dutch Colony* and then five other examples in the book *New York as an English Colony.*
Drama!	**DARE to Compare!**	**Colonial Sites**
You will perform a one-person character play. Grab the spotlight and a book (Sarah Morton or Samuel Eaton) and tell your story (read it aloud) as if you were a Pilgrim child growing up in 1627. Practice, practice, practice, and perhaps you'll get a chance to record your play!	Compare & contrast Colonial school days to today's school days. Read "Colonial Schools" (an article) and *Colonial Teachers* (a book) to help.	Visit some Colonial web sites where you can learn more about this fascinating time in our history. Record five new facts you've learned and let us know if you'd recommend this site to your classmates!

Figure 2.6. Menu Variation on Tic-Tac-Toe Board

The Roman Rotisserie

Where History is Made

Menu

Name _____

Date _____

Teacher _____

Directions: You will contract for a grade for this unit by choosing several items from the menu to "eat" over a three-week period.

Requirements & Information:

- Select menu items from *each* category to complete. Categories include *geography*, *government*, *vocabulary*, *culture*, and *technology*.
- Choose items based on their point value and your interests and talents.
- The maximum number of points you can earn for this project is 300. Complete the assignments necessary to receive the maximum number of points.
- Circle the items on the menu that you choose to complete. Use this as your assignment guide.

The Roman Rotisserie

Due Date: _____

Grade for the Unit: _____

Point System:

Appetizers	$10
Entrées	$20
Desserts	$10
Beverages	$ 5

Sample 3-Week Menu:

Monday:	Appetizer	$10
	Beverage	$ 5
Tuesday:	Entrée	$20
Wednesday:	Entrée	$20
Thursday:	Appetizer	$10
	Appetizer	$10
Friday:	Entrée	$20
Monday:	Entrée	$20
Tuesday:	Appetizer	$10
	Beverage	$ 5
	Dessert	$10
Wednesday:	Entrée	$20
Thursday:	Dessert	$10
Friday:	Dessert	$10
	Beverage	$ 5
Monday:	Appetizer	$10
Tuesday:	Entrée	$20
Wednesday:	Dessert	$10
Thursday:	Beverage	$ 5
	Beverage	$ 5
Friday:	Entrée	$20

Total	$225

(out of 300) = 85%

—Hours—
Monday–Friday—During Class Time
Studyhall & 10th Period

Appetizer   *$10*
1) "Roman Life – Numbers" worksheet
2) Compare Family Life – fill in the chart
3) Write a persuasive letter to the editor on behalf of women or slaves supporting their right to vote.

Entrée   *$20*
1) The Best Gods? – read and compare! Write a paragraph to support your decision.
2) Read Chapter 7, Section 4 in the Ancient World Textbook. Complete the activities.
3) Choose ten words from this unit and make a "pictionary" of them.

Dessert $10
1) "How Much Latin Do You Know?"
2) Interview with a Gladiator
3) Draw a picture and label features in Roman home

Beverage   *$ 5*
1) "Roman Life—Entertainment" worksheet
2) "Roman Life—Public Baths" worksheet
3) Color and label the map

Appetizer   *$10*
1) "Fill in the God and Goddesses " chart
2) "Ancient Rome" matching worksheet
3) Where did the Roman Empire Start?" sheet

Modified version of a menu variation on the Tic-Tac-Toe Board originally created by Susan Cappello. Reprinted with permission.

Literacy Bin activities help to motivate students by addressing a variety of learning styles and a range of modalities that may be difficult to integrate within your language arts instruction. For example, activities could be shaped to better align with the learning styles most commonly associated with Howard Gardner's multiple-intelligences theory:

- *Logical/Mathematical Intelligence*—The literacy activity would include some form of student participation through numbers, calculations, mathematical situations, events, and functions or other numeral-based activities, such as solving mathematical word problems or designing structures using some mathematical parameters.

- *Verbal/Linguistic*—The literacy activity would incorporate writing or speaking, such as Reader's Theater or crafting a poem.

- *Visual/Spatial*—The activity would include color, shapes, patterns, and other dominantly visual components, such as a photographic essay or a collage.

- *Bodily/Kinesthetic*—Activities would involve movement or hands-on participation, such as a pantomime act or dance.

- *Musical*—Activities that call for music or tonal patterns, such as creating a rap or metered poem or even constructing a device to make music, would be added.

- *Interpersonal*—A pair or team of students might be involved in an activity, such as a Reader's Theater play or a debate on a controversial issue.

- *Intrapersonal*—This intelligence would focus on the inner states of being, self-recognition, and metacognition, including self-reflected activities such as a monologue (or soliloquy).

- *Naturalist*—Activities would include elements of nature or the environment, such as collecting and identifying leaves or materials used to construct an animal's home. Environmental matters could also be incorporated into these activities.

Our intent in introducing the Literacy Bin activities into our literacy instruction was to encourage students to participate in other types of activities that would support their learning once they had completed their daily instructional reading assignments. The Literacy Bin activities presented unique opportunities for students to work in different types of configurations, such as in pairs or clusters of three or more students, and to build their understanding and skills in unique ways. Activities used included performing Reader's Theater, writing poetry or songs, drawing pictures, and writing and illustrating comic books. As our objective was to help students build background knowledge and to encourage them to practice and strengthen the reading strategies, the activities we included in our Literacy Bins involved reading in addition to other forms of the literary expression, such as writing, speaking, and listening, and even computer activities, such as blogging and creating web casts.

Creating your own Literacy Bin or similar assortment of literacy activities isn't complicated. Pulling together materials (discussed below) and then organizing the activities using a simple system for students to follow is all that's necessary. Keep in mind, however, that these activities *supplement* instruction. They are not intended to replace it, nor do they provide students with the same level of teacher guidance that is offered in small group instruction.

A Peek into the Classroom

Mrs. White sat at a table working with seven students who, for several days, were reading a news magazine article about the Erie Canal. She had just asked students to share the main ideas they had identified from their assigned reading passages and had recorded in their Read-Along Guide. Meanwhile, four students who took the "library pass" from one compartment in the Literacy Bin had just left the classroom to practice "Capers on the Canal," a Reader's Theater play about children growing up on the canal. Another group of three students were assembled on carpet squares near the front of the room. They were drawing a map of the canal and working with reading materials and calculators that had been obtained from the Literacy Bin. Two students sat at their own desks, one working on a crossword puzzle and the other on a word search. Both activities contained vocabulary words and definitions that related to the Erie Canal. Five students who had recently finished the small-group instructional time with Mrs. White were completing their practice activities, finding main idea and support details from their book *The Amazing Impossible Erie Canal* (Harness, 1999). Once students completed their activities, they would select activities to complete from their tic-tac-toe board.

Methods for Monitoring

Teachers have a great deal of flexibility in determining the types of activities they wish to feature in their Literacy Bin. They also have much flexibility in determining the degree to which they wish to monitor and/or assess their students' performance on the activities. Teachers can make their own methods, based on their own objectives. Some teachers with whom we've worked do the following:

♦ *A Quick Check*—The teacher initials the student's game board after having provided a quick check of the student's work. This may be done after a student completes one activity or after a given number of activities. During this quick check, the teacher is scanning the work for accuracy, quality, and completion. As is clear from Figure 2.7, a quick check provides students with a reminder of the teacher's expectations. You may wish to have student define in their own words the performance criteria.

Figure 2.7. A Quick Check System

```
┌─────────────────────────────────────────────────────────────┐
│                    Literacy Bin Activities                    │
│                                                               │
│  A_ = Accurate  Be sure your content information is correct.  │
│                                                               │
│  Quick = Quality Work  This work should be "Best Effort"      │
│                         quality.                              │
│                                                               │
│  Check = Complete  Be sure you completed all parts of the     │
│                     activity.                                 │
└─────────────────────────────────────────────────────────────┘
```

♦ *Literacy Bin Observation*—The teacher periodically observes students participating in the Literacy Bin activities. Monitoring students for appropriate behavior, their ability to self-select activities, their pacing in completing activities, their skills working both independently as well as in teams, and their ability to work in an environment with little teacher support are examples of criteria. Figure 2.8 is a sample observation form. Teachers may determine what criteria they wish to monitor based on their objectives.

Figure 2.8. Literacy Bin Observation Form

```
┌───────────────────────────────────────────────────────────────┐
│ Literacy Bin Observation on Kevin Wong Date Mar. 12            │
│ (Review tic-tac-toe board & completed projects)                │
│                                                                │
│   ♦ Demonstrates appropriate behavior (X) Yes   ( ) No         │
│                                                                │
│   ♦ Selects Activities Appropriately (X) Yes   ( ) No          │
│                                                                │
│   ♦ Appropriate Pacing (X) Yes   ( ) No                        │
│                                                                │
│   ♦ Works Well in Teams & Independently (X) Yes   ( ) No       │
│                                                                │
│   ♦ Self-Sufficient (X) Yes   ( ) No                           │
│                                                                │
│ Comments Kevin has made great progress from the start of the   │
│ school year. He has learned how to work on his own, and he can │
│ now successfully monitor his attention and focus. Great job,   │
│ Kevin!                                                         │
└───────────────────────────────────────────────────────────────┘
```

♦ *Portfolio Checklist*—Students select one activity from those they completed and include it in a Literacy Bin Portfolio. The teacher may wish to help students determine how to select an activity by providing them with a checklist like the one shown in Figure 2.9. This checklist aligns with other monitoring components used with the Literacy Bins, such as the Quick Check, and encourages students to base their selection on some criteria. As is also evident from the checklist, it incorporates elements that are linked to the overall motivation improvement initiative, such as a focus on best-effort practices.

Figure 2.9. Literacy Bin Portfolio Checklist

Mackenzie Joiner's Literacy Bin Portfolio Checklist

Bin The Colonial Period   Date February 5

The work I've selected for my portfolio is:

(X) Accurate, Quality Work, Complete!

(X) Represents my Best Efforts!

(X) Unique—there's no activity like it in my portfolio!

(X) Work That Makes Me Proud!

I wanted to share this work because:

I thought that this word search was one of the harder ones in the Bins we've done so far. I had to search letter by letter. I think I can spell every word now!

Solutions to Keep in Mind

◆ *Frequency*—Because the Literacy Bins are aligned with the instructional units in our language arts curriculum, we use them whenever we provide our small-group strategy-based comprehension instruction. At times, we have combined themes in the Literacy Bins, such as including activities on both the *Revolutionary War Period* and *The New Nation and Government*. This allows students more time to complete activities in the Bin, especially if their instructional reading lessons are weighty and they do not have much time to work on the supplementary activities. Instead of replacing a Bin after two to three weeks, such as during the *Revolutionary War* unit, the combined Literacy Bin remains in place for four to six weeks. Teachers may wish to encourage students to work on activities that align with the content of their instruction, or they may wish to challenge students by having them select activities in the unit that is forthcoming.

◆ *Activities should not require the need for teacher assistance*—Although teachers may need to introduce activities when a new Bin is made available, this should be the only time teacher assistance is necessary. As the teacher is typically involved in small-group instruction, the teacher should not be disturbed by students working on the Bin activities. As such, not only do the activities need to be prepared keeping this in mind, but classroom routines so students can be self-sufficient need to be established. Introducing and briefly explaining the activities in a Literacy Bin will be needed. Including all materials needed to complete an activity in the Bin or letting students know where they may find the materials, such as in a classroom art cabinet, will also be needed. Encouraging students to quietly help one another builds their self-sufficiency and promotes teamwork.

♦ *Teachers may wish to direct some students to particular activities*—Teachers might decide that certain students would benefit from practice with specific activities. For example, some students may need to strengthen their content vocabulary and would benefit from an activity such as a crossword puzzle, matching activity, or a word search. Highlighting the game board where the activity appears is one way to accomplish this. In other cases, a more formal agreement, such as an activity contract that is completed jointly between the student and the teacher, could be used. Student contracts are discussed in Chapter 4.

♦ *Differentiated starting points and expectations*—There's no harm in creating activities that may seem to cater to the interests of a particular student, especially if little else seems to engage the student. It has been our experience that although we may have created an activity to align with the interests of a particular student, other students also selected, enjoyed, and benefited from the activity. Chances are an activity that attracts one student will attract other students. Likewise, as teachers are reviewing student performance on activities, they may vary their expectations based on the range of their students' skills and abilities.

A Peek into the Classroom

Chen's baseball card collection filled multiple binders, which he carted back and forth to school in his backpack. His cards were his source of enjoyment, and his teacher tried working together with Chen so he'd be able to play with them at recess time, instead of having to catch up on his homework in study hall. Despite this understanding, Chen struggled to stay caught up with class assignments and he continued to have much trouble completing his homework regularly. The work was hard for him and, although he realized he had to use more effort, he seemed unable to get out from under a cycle that perpetually left him behind. When his teacher introduced the Literacy Bin, aligned to the unit on Native Americans, Chen was intrigued by an activity that involved making trading cards on well-known Native Americans. He wanted to do that activity and felt it was something he'd be good at. He regained his determination.

♦ *Students may need some support with the process of self-selecting activities*—Some intermediate-level students may not have much experience selecting activities on their own. Assuming that a student will know how to select an activity and then work independently toward completing it is not something that all students can master without some guidance. Monitoring this, especially at the start of your use of the Literacy Bins, will quickly enable you to assist those students who are inexperienced with this.

♦ *Locating/creating materials for the Bin activities*—Begin with materials you already have and create around them. For example, review any and all materials you've collected over time that align with your curriculum, such as activities, reading passages, and news articles. Determine ways in which these materials might be used in a bin activity, and supplement them as necessary, such as by creating charts to accompany them or by combining them with other items. You can also review your school's book collections and determine new ways in which students could work with those materials, such as by performing Reader's Theater using characters' dialogue. Your librarian might also be a good resource for ideas and/or assistance. As the bin activities align with the content in your language arts instruction, chances are they'll be used from one year to the next. This enables you to build, replace, and improve your Bins from year to year. If you are new to teaching, working with a team of teachers, such as a grade-level team or even a cross-grade-level team, will make this process easier.

♦ *Determining a comfortable "noise level"*—Just as you will want to build "self-sufficiency" into your bin activities, you may also want to consider the noise level of the activities you include. Remembering that you will often be instructing a group of students while others are involved in the bin activities, you may want to determine an acceptable noise level where both types of events can occur simultaneously without causing distractions. Still, if some activities may require a level of participation that could be distracting to others (such as drama or fluency activities), you might be able to arrange other accommodation for small groups of students. For example, students may be able to work in your library when instruction is not taking place there under the librarian's supervision. Similarly, you may be able to provide other supervised opportunities outside of your classroom.

♦ *Seeking help from volunteers and other school professionals*—Depending on your school's policy, you might seek outside volunteers to help with small groups of students either in the classroom, while you're working with a reading group, or even in other locations within your school. Some students may need extra time and support to complete tasks and working with volunteers and other school professionals may be one solution to help accommodate this need.

♦ *Reviewing student work and sharing activities*—Students want to share their activities and should be encouraged to do so as a way of demonstrating that the activities are important and valued. Still, finding the time may be tricky.

Some teachers use brief intervals of time between activities, such as between recess and their next class, to allow students to share their activities and also to do a quick check for students. An alternative would be to schedule a small block of time on a weekly basis for sharing. Displaying the work in the classroom, in a hallway, or in the entry way to the school is another way to share the activities.

♦ *Rewards*—In following with the popular tic-tac-toe game, students are often awarded a small prize for completing any type of row. Many teachers choose to use practical school supplies for rewards, while others select prizes that are more novel, such as a small toy or a treat. The key is to provide a selection of prizes that will encourage and reward students.

Other Ideas for Literacy Bins

♦ Specific skills can also be practiced in the Bins. For example, featuring activities that allow students to practice the common rules for spelling is one way the bins could be used to strengthen a particular skill. Packaged materials, such as those involving word sorts or word construction activities, are another possibility. Even something as basic as handwriting can become the subject for multiple activities.

♦ Test preparation is another area that could be practiced through Bin activities. Standardized state tests generally feature multiple-choice questions as well as some element of writing. Creating Bins that can be used to review content as well as simple test preparation procedures, such as reminders for reading all responses to multiple choice questions before selecting a response, might enliven this process.

♦ Designing Bin activities to feature well-liked activities that span curriculum areas, such as Reader's Theater or poetry, is another very popular approach.

♦ A special theme, such as an author visit, could also be a topic for a Literacy Bin.

Wrap-up on Literacy Bins

Using Literacy Bin activities to supplement language arts instructions by giving students unique opportunities to learn in new ways and to participate in shaping their own learning is one way to get students engaged. The activities might be the spark that ignites some students, and the fuel that intensifies the efforts of others. Determining when and how you wish to use Literacy Bins are matters you can judge best. Integrating them within your curriculum enables students to use them confidently and with ease, even if you choose to vary the types of Bins you use. In addition to recognizing that these are excellent tools for motivation, they also help students build their fluency and their background knowledge.

Mini Book Clubs

Over the past several years, classroom book clubs have gained popularity and present teachers and students with new avenues to engage in reading activities. Many of us are familiar with different types of book clubs, having seen them used in many ways: book publishers use them as a marketing concept to sell books; schools offer summer reading clubs to encourage children to read when school is not in session; libraries host them, bringing people together who share common interests; and television personalities host them on a national level and provide participants with numerous means of sharing in discussions. And even more, newer trends continue with electronic book clubs, mother–daughter clubs, father–son clubs, and so on. This near shape-shifting power of "the book club" suggested to us that the format could help us with our motivation improvement plans.

The way in which we integrated the book club format into our reading activities was to incorporate *mini book clubs* into our language arts instruction. Unique features of these mini clubs include:

- ♦ They were roughly four to five days long.
- ♦ Selections included high-interest, small-format books that spanned a variety of reading levels (nonfiction).
- ♦ From seven to ten offerings were made available.
- ♦ Students selected the book they wished to read.
- ♦ Reading groups were heterogeneous.
- ♦ Discussion was encouraged among students during practice time.
- ♦ Specific topics within our strategy-based comprehension instruction were used during the mini book clubs.

Our intent in introducing the mini book club into our reading approach was to add some novelty and variety to our conventional instructional format. In the book clubs, we encouraged students to choose a book on a topic of interest to them. Likewise, our typical homogeneous grouping configurations gave way to random grouping. This enabled students to work with others whom they might not have worked with before. We provided the same strategy-based comprehension instruction as in the past, only we selected lessons that could easily accommodate juggling up to seven texts; we were mindful of our preparation time and also the amount of direct instruction and teacher support that would be available with up to seven groups.

The reading levels of the texts comprising our selection ranged from N to S (Fountas & Pinnell classification for middle third-grade to late fourth-grade text gradients). We recognized that some students would select works that extended beyond their instructional reading level, whereas others would select works that were below their instructional level. Still, all of the nonfiction books we selected contained varied avenues for learning, such as photographs, sidebars, and maps. These features would help students who were reading a text that was above their level. Additionally, the topics the texts covered were considered "high interest," which would hold the attention of those reading a text that was mildly too high or too low for their reading level. Moreover, students could confer and discuss ideas together while they were practicing their reading comprehension strategies. We believed that the stronger readers could serve as peer coaches for others who might be confused by the content (which we would further clarify during small-group instructional time). Also, the knowledge each member could contribute to the discussions during their practice time could help build their understanding of the material. Our thinking was that if students were interested in a topic, they most likely knew something about it and could contribute this knowledge during discussions. Still, each student was responsible for their own unique thinking and their own responses in their Read-Along Guide. With all of these systems in place, we felt confident that the approach could enable all students to succeed despite the elements that we recognized were contrary to conventional wisdom.

Figure 2.10 (page 50) is an Instructional Unit Plan for a Mini Book Club on "A Selection of Comprehension Strategies," which included Making Connections, Visualizing to Support the Text, Asking Questions to Engage in the Text, and Building Vocabulary Using Context Clues. Nine titles are listed and daily reading assignments provided for the five titles selected by the students (students made their own assignments). Key activities for "before," "during," and "after" instruction are also included. Because we structured each of our lessons using a Read-Along Guide (discussed in Chapter 1), we included only brief notes in our Instructional Unit Plan. Figure 2.11 (page 51) features a selection of pages from a Mini Book Club Read-Along Guide. Other themes that we've used this format for include "Exploring the Use of Comprehension Strategies in Nonfiction" and "Introduction to Nonfiction Features." There certainly could be many others.

(Text continues on page 52.)

Figure 2.10. Instructional Unit Plan for a Mini Book Club

Instructional Unit Plan – Mini Book Club

Theme: _Selection of Comprehension Strategies_ Strategies: _Making Connections, Visualizing, Asking Questions, Vocabulary_

Chapter Breakout: (Title/Level)

1. Welcome to the I.S.S. (Logan)	2. West by Stagecoach (Thompson)	3. Volcanologists (Kraft)	4. Saving the Florida Panther (Offinoski)	5. Amazing Arachnids (Floyd)
P. 4-7		P. 4-8	P. 2-7	P. 4-6
P. 8-14		P. 9-13	P. 8-13	P. 7-9
P. 15-19		P. 14-18	P. 14-19	P. 10-15
P. 20-21		P. 19-23	P. 20-21	P. 16-19
P. 22-23				P. 21-23

6. Growing Up with Music (Murphy)	7. Matthew Brady (Offinoski)	8. I Could Not Keep Silent (Meeker)	9. True Heroes (Fuerst)	10.
		P. 4-8		
		P. 9-14		
		P. 15-22		
		P. 23-28		

Instructional Plans

Before	During	After
Review student groups, use of strategies for nonfiction. Introduce books briefly + browse time	Reading + recording in Read-Along Guide. Independent, paired or shared reading. Collaborative sharing in guide.	After each cluster of pages, students to share responses + highlights of strategy use.

Notes on Read-Along Guide Use:
Students can break-up page clusters – assign or discuss strategy prompts

Figure 2.11. Read-Along Guide for Mini Book Club

_____'s Mini Book Club Read-Along Guide

Title: I Could Not Keep Silent

Author: Clare Hodgson Meeker

I selected this book because the title popped out at me and I have always enjoyed a good biography. The cover also had a cover picture that I thought was interesting.

Strategy Practice

In this Read-Along Guide we will practice:

1. Making Connections.
2. Visualizing to Support the Text.(pictures)
3. Asking Questions to Engage in the Text.(questions)
4. Building Vocabulary Using Context Clues.

1. Making Connections

Good readers use prior knowledge and experiences to better understand what they're reading. Sometimes it's helpful to think about how you know or "connect with" a character, event, or some part of the passage or book you're reading. Your connection could be any of these three: Text-to-Self Connection (T-S), Text-to-Text Connection (T-T), or Text-to-World Connection (T-W). Sometimes it's hard to make connections when you're reading nonfiction, especially if your book is about a person who is very different from you, or if it's about a place you've never been, or if it's about an event you're learning about for the first time. But it's important to try your best!

Directions: Let's practice thinking about connections we make during our reading. Use the prompt below to record your connection and label T-S, T-T, or T-W to identify what type of connection you've made.

When I Read Page #	I Thought About...	Type of Connection
5	how I am like Rachel because I enjoy animals and the enviroment.	T-S
6	how I also enjoy to be outside with my dogs Hampton and Mia.	T-S
11	what if would be like if you had to sell your family china like Rachel.	T-S
12	disecting a frog like Rachel had to do in her required class, biology	T-S
13	when I go to the ocean and stand in the tides like Rachel did.	T-S
14	a stormy night like the one Rachel sat in at her college.	T-S
All	I'd be against pestisides like Rachel.	T-W
28	how bad I would feel if I had cancer.	T-S

2

4. Build Vocabulary Using Context Clues

Being able to figure out the meaning of new or unfamiliar words as you read is a really important but hard skill to master. It's kind of like good detective work where you try and work with clues in the text. It takes a lot of practice but imagine never being stumped by a word again! There are seven methods that can help you:

1. "Sound Out" the word - you might know it when you say it.
2. "Chunk" the word - is there a root word, a prefix, or suffix?
3. Link the word to a known word - does it look like another word you know?
4. Look for smaller words you recognize - is the word a compound word?
5. Use context clues - use clues from surrounding sentences.
6. Think about what makes sense - ask yourself 'What would make sense?'
7. Others - ask a teacher, use a dictionary, use a glossary.

Directions: Use the space below to write your new or unfamiliar word. Then, try to use one or more of the methods to figure out the meaning. Be sure to list the number of the method you used and give a definition of the word.

New or Unfamiliar Word	Method(s) Used	Definition
contaminated	6	made harmful + unusable
pestisides	5	Chemical products used to destroy plants, fungal, or animal pests!
ecology	6	The relationship of all living things and their enviroment.
fossilized	5	Things that have died and developed into a fossil.
civil service exam	6	A test given to a person who is wanting into a government job.
ecosystem	5	A community within the enviroment
frustration	1	angry, mad
disastrous	2	a disaster

8

My Reading Response Journal

Possible Ideas For Your Journal Entries Could Be:

1. What was going through your mind as you read this?
2. How did you feel while reading this part?
3. What questions did your have when you finished reading?
4. What are the one or two most important ideas?
5. Make predictions about the next reading.
6. What would you do if this happened to you?
7. How are you similar to one of the characters?
8. Other

Pages __14__ to __21__ Date __6/24__

My response to today's reading is I still think this book does not have anything to do with the title. I am guessing it has to do with a book she wrote. I thought it was very happy how Rachel got to see the ocean. I thought it was mean how Rachel's sisters two young daugters needed help and Rachel's brother Robert offered no help. That is my response to today's reading.

Pages __22__ to __31__ Date __6/26__

My response to today's reading is these pages were sad. First of all, Rachel Carson slowly dies from cancer. It is sad to see someone go away like that. What is even more interesting is when Rachel still fights against DDT which is pesticide. She was a remarkable woman. That is my response to today's reading.

7

A Peek into the Classroom

Mrs. Donovan stopped to chat with a group of four students who chose to sit at the table in the back of the classroom. They were reading *If We Had Wings: The Story of the Tuskegee Airmen*, having selected the book because of their mutual interest in wartime. The students had been practicing the strategies of Visualizing and Making Connections and were now sharing their examples. Ben, Jessup, and Aubrey had asked Wesley for help with a tricky passage, which they agreed they would mark with a sticky note despite thinking that with Wesley's help their understanding was clear. They planned to check their understanding with Mrs. Donovan when it was their turn for her to visit. Mrs. Donovan patiently listened as the boys described how Wesley helped them get the meaning of the passage. Groups of other students were working together throughout the classroom, some reading from their books, others recording information, and still others discussing their books.

Methods for Monitoring

For numerous reasons, we typically don't monitor or assess students during the mini book clubs as we would for our more traditional instructional reading units (discussed in Chapter 1); the units are short, students are encouraged to discuss and share ideas, the degree to which students contribute background knowledge is intangible, among other issues. However, some teachers might choose to include some form of informal survey, such as the one in Figure 2.12, where students share their ideas on the successes or weaknesses of the mini book clubs. Some teachers believe this is more in keeping with the friendly, want-to-participate tone they desire for their book clubs. Teachers could use a rubric or some type of checklist. Working with project-based activities such as having students perform commercials or write brochures about their books are other alternatives. During the small-group instruction, teachers can readily grasp whether or not students struggle with concepts. Also, if the lessons used within the mini book club format are selected because they are not complicated and will be revisited during the year; therefore, the need to formally assess students may not be necessary.

Figure 2.12. Penny-for-Your-Thoughts Survey

Name ___George Jackson___   Date _____May 19_____

A Penny For Your Thoughts

On the ___Nonfiction – Special Interest___ **Mini Book Club!**

1. List the strategies you practiced during the Mini Book Club:

1. Making Connections?

2. Visualizing to Support the Text

3. Asking Questions to Engage in the Text.

4. Building Vocabulary Using Context Clues.

Which strategy was the most challenging for you? ___Building Vocabulary___

Which strategy was the least challenging for you? ___Visualizing___

2. Do you feel using these strategies helped you with your comprehension?

Yes, I feel using these strategies helped with my comprehension because I didn't know much about spiders. I didn't even know what the word "Arachnids" meant. I also didn't know there were so many. Adding onto what I did know and Visualizing helped me learn more.

3. Did you enjoy working with others? Do you feel the group was successful helping one another?

Yes, I enjoyed working with my friends, especially Elliot and Suzanne. Suzanne helped me figure out some hard words. She's good at that! Elliot and I learned a lot from each other when we shared the pictures we had about the types of spiders. It was great!

4. What did you enjoy most about this Mini Book Club?

I liked picking my own book to read and I liked reading with my friends. Also it was fun trying to figure out the hard words, because I knew that Suzanne would be able to help me.

5. What changes would you make to the next Mini Book Club?

I think we should have more books to read about the same subjects. Like I would pick another book about spiders because I want to learn more about them now. I know Jason wants to learn about them now.

Solutions to Keep in Mind

♦ *Frequency*—Although the mini book club format is typically used only for instruction in two reading comprehension units, it could be used more often for a variety of purposes. The section *Other Ideas for Mini Book Clubs* below provides some suggestions. Certainly, the frequency with which they are used will be determined based on your goals.

♦ *Working well with others*—Encouraging students to discuss their ideas and share their experiences and background knowledge on a topic without the direct supervision of a teacher may be a new thing for some. Providing easy-to-follow parameters and establishing some guidelines may be needed. Many teachers find that the general classroom management expectations and procedures they set up at the start of the school year work well and need only to remind students of them before beginning the mini book clubs.

♦ *Creativity and locating materials*—Finding multiple copies of some books may take some crafty troubleshooting skills. Launching your mini book clubs with materials you already have in your collections might be the best starting point. Consider working with electronic sites that enable you to download e-books, such as A to Z Books (*www.a-zreading.org*). Other options include working with textbooks, newsmagazines, basal readers, and other materials you might not typically consider for your small-group reading instruction. Working with grade-level colleagues, as well as your school librarians and your local libraries (both of which usually have access to larger networks of libraries), might be another avenue to take when trying to track multiple copies of specific books. Building your own collections will take some time.

♦ *Sorry, not interested!*—Some students may not be interested in any of the available books. Should this occur, you might wish to keep a collection of books that could easily serve as substitutes. Keeping in mind that too much choice may be distracting and/or overwhelming to some students, offering from three to five substitutes might be best. Still, encouraging students to work in small groups so they can benefit from peer modeling, background knowledge, and shared discussion, should be a priority when working with this format.

♦ *Can't stop now!*—Students often wish to continue reading and learning more about their topic of interest, or to continue working in this manner with friends who share the same interests. Although you might not choose to include additional mini book clubs in your plans, you could encourage students to read independently and even possibly coordinate their extra reading by meeting other goals such as the reading mandates that most states now include as a component of their curriculum standards. Working with your school or local librarian to provide additional listings of appropriate titles available on a subject is a resourceful way in which to connect students with books. Gleaning the insights of those most familiar with vast collections as well as new titles will be helpful.

♦ *Rewards*—Most teachers don't reward students for their involvement in the mini book clubs. Allowing students to add the book they read to a classroom reading list or a state-mandated reading list is sometimes the best motivation. Most students agree that the exciting discussion that takes place during instructional time and working together with friends are rewards enough. As stated throughout, using your judgment on matters of rewards is your best guide.

Other Ideas for Mini Book Clubs

♦ One of our objectives for using the mini book clubs was to introduce students to applying comprehension strategies to nonfiction. Another was to help students begin to distinguish between features that are unique to nonfiction. There are many possibilities of using the clubs for this purpose that will align with a variety of content areas, such as Athletes/Sports, Presidents, Discoveries, Explorers, Biographies, Poetry/Poets, Periods of Time in History, Heroes, and Inventors.

♦ Determining other objectives of mini book club lesson(s) is a matter of choice. Objectives such as understanding sequencing, grasping the main idea, comparing and contrasting, and others suitable for strategy-based comprehension instruction will also work. Using this format to introduce various genres is another avenue to take.

♦ Using the clubs to assist students with the process of self-selecting texts and working through criteria that might help them with this process is another.

♦ With the recent trend of working with picture books at any grade level, including multiple copies of these or illustrated story books (the latter of which generally includes more text) is another source that could provide variety and novelty to your reading program. Here, too, units coordinated to the language arts curriculum could just as easily work as those connected to science, social studies, art, and others.

Wrap-up on Mini Book Clubs

Now, more than ever, considering new and unique ways to use your small-group skills seems ideal. Teachers and students are gaining some degree of comfort with this format. Additionally, publishers are exploring new ways to attract readers. For example they're producing new formats, such as the small-format books, graphic informational novels, comics, and Reader's Theater plays. These types of products are available on a variety of topics, and there are even works referred to as "Hi-Los," which are books considered to be high interest and low vocabulary and readability. Using the clubs to incorporate these new and trendier types of books into your small-group reading offers students unique ways to engage in reading. Likewise, providing students with a wider range of "choice" and an ability to make their own selection might enable some to spotlight their background knowledge in new ways.

Self-Monitoring for Continuous Improvement

We began encouraging students to monitor elements of their reading performance based on the success one of our colleagues had when his students began to track their own progress on several state practice assessments. What he found was that once students began following their progress, they intrinsically worked harder to show improvement. These findings have since been supported by our own activities and classroom studies. (Athans, Devine, Henry, Parente, & Sammon, 2006). We were also encouraged by the fact that this outcome was consistently true among nearly all students; wanting to "beat" a previous score and even setting challenging goals for future performance were common reactions among most students.

After studying factors to determine why this was so, we arrived at four explanations:

1. Encouraging students to take the time to do something sends the immediate message that the activity is important. Although we believe that all literacy-based activities—reading, writing, speaking, listening, as well as the critical thinking processes that underlie, bridge, and connect all literacies—are important and valuable, to assume that all of our students share in this belief is misguided (see Chapter 1). Encouraging students not only to spend time engaged in these activities but to also monitor their participation firmly supports the idea that the literacy activities are important and that success is valued.

2. Keeping in mind the age and typical activities of our intermediate-level learners, we are reminded that they may not have had much experience assuming responsibility and accountability. Obviously, some will have more experience than others, just as surely as some will demonstrate a propensity to assume it more readily than others. Still, students may need ongoing instruction, nurturing, and guidance to grasp these ideals. Self-monitoring their progress on academic tasks often introduces students to the concept that they are, in part, responsible and accountable for their academic progress.

3. Once students develop an interest in self-monitoring their activities, they also seem to want to take charge of what happens to them—they want to participate in their success. When this transition happens, our job becomes showing them how to do this, removing barriers to their success, and supporting them onward.

4. Through the use of monitoring devices to help students track their progress, students are also inadvertently provided with a differentiated action plan to improve achievement. Each student soon becomes aware of his or her

strengths as well as areas needing improvement. Recognizing this becomes the starting point for positive change.

The benefits of the self-monitoring technique helped build student motivation. Still, we also recognized that special precautions needed to be in place. We wanted to build and strengthen students' skills, yet remain mindful of the fragility of their self-image. At times, this required a careful balancing act. Likewise, we wanted students to tackle challenges both as part of a classroom community and independently, without treading on issues of privacy, such as posting grades.

A Peek into the Classroom

Hillary took her chart from the pocket of her reading folder and scanned the graph where she had charted her performance on her multiple-choice assessments. She had graphed all four assessments she had since the beginning of the school year and was now eager to see the results of the recent test that Ms. Halloway was currently returning. She had scored progressively better on each test and hoped her extra effort to carefully review her answers on this last test would continue the upward trend.

William was looking over his chart, thinking about how he used to rush through his tests, often picking answers without reading them carefully. He sometimes changed his answers if he felt he'd already picked a certain lettered response too many times in a row. He remembered after plotting the discouraging results from his second test, that he had made up his mind to work harder to use his reading strategies. He glanced at the third plot, which showed much improvement, and remembered how happy he was to see that his effort paid off. On this last test, he not only used his reading strategies, but he also went back to the stories to find support for the answers he had selected. He felt confident that this last test would show even better results.

Methods for Monitoring

Teachers who have chosen to incorporate self-monitoring systems within their literacy activities use a variety of methods. Some use line graphs to monitor changes over time, such as the one shown in Figure 2.13 (page 58), which features a student's scores on similar types of assessments. Here the student monitors her progress on five assessments, each containing twenty-eight multiple-choice questions. Other teachers have used double bar graphs if students are asked to first predict an outcome and then chart the actual outcome. Using graphs is one way for students to quickly grasp their progress over time and are especially useful for tracking data such as correct responses on multiple-choice, matching, short-answer, and other forms of objective activities or assessments.

Figure 2.13. Line Graph of Student Self-Monitoring Device

Name: Emily Manion

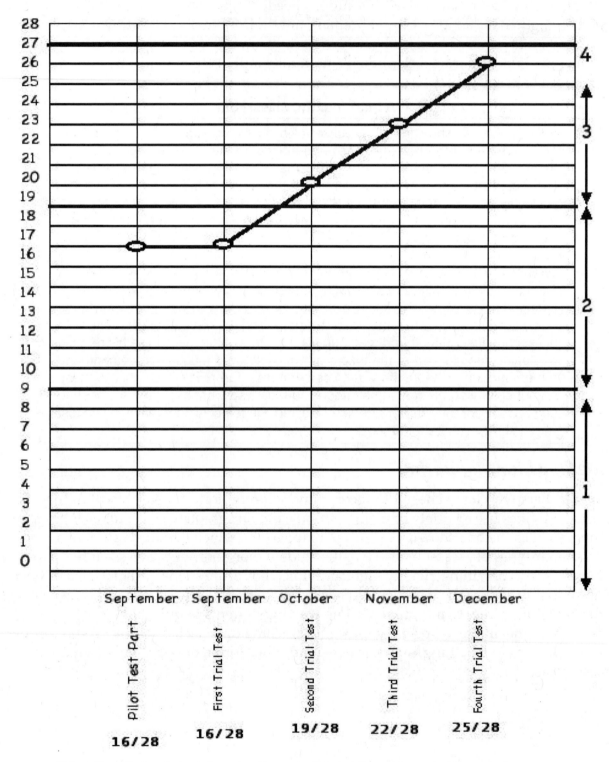

This self-monitoring device is based on the work of Kevin Ellis and is used with permission.

Another method often used for written activities or assessments is tracking charts that highlight key factors or traits over the course of times. Figure 2.14 (page 60) is a sample of a Personal Writing Plan where students recorded *strengths* and *areas of development* for their writing pieces based on the districtwide writing rubric used by their teacher. Students reviewed their grades in each of the four categories, noting strengths and areas needing development. As the teacher reviewed strong papers and modeled how to strengthen others during whole-class review, students noted ways in which they could improve their own work. These plans were kept in a writing binder together with their papers and were quickly reviewed by students at the onset of every writing assignment so they would benefit from this self-reflective process.

For tracking student activities that are posted, teachers might wish to use individual charts or one chart that contains each student's name. Deciding which will work best is largely a matter of personal preference.

Solutions to Keep in Mind

♦ *Frequency*—Determining the frequency for using this strategy is a matter of personal preference, yet your decision as to when and where to use it may largely be based on the available materials or methods you currently have in place to accommodate it. For example, if you already use standardized activities, assessments, or other materials within your literacy-based activities, you'll have no trouble incorporating these with this approach. On the other hand, it may be necessary for you to mildly alter some materials should you wish to develop a device in which students can track their continuous improvement over time.

♦ *Balancing your students' wish for (and protection of) privacy with their need for celebration*—You should consider which forms of self-monitoring devices to display and which ones students should maintain in their personal folders. Teachers often display tracking devices for activities in which students are successful. On the other hand, teachers will often ask students to keep charts that contain test scores or grades in their individual folders and will further remind students that their grades are private, and like report cards, need not be shared with others. This also reinforces the idea that student are challenging themselves and are not comparing their progress to that of their classmates.

♦ *Discouraging fluctuations: matters of content fairness*—Sometimes students might be disappointed by scores that fluctuate. Our experience is that fluctuations might be the result of the content. For example, students tracking their progress on a language arts assessment might perform better on a test covering tall tales than on a test given twenty weeks later covering government. Despite the fact that the students had twenty additional weeks to practice and strengthen their comprehension strategies, they still had trouble maintaining or progressing on their scores because of the increasingly

Figure 2.14. Personal Writing Plan for Self-Monitoring

Personal Writing Plan

Name _Alexandra Grayson_   Date _November 15_

So Far, I Have Written:

1. _Friendly Letter Home to Parents_
2. _Character Traits of Thomas Alva Edison_
3. _Compare/Contrast Essay for Two Fables_
4. _Persuasive Letter to Principal Jones_
5. _Personal Narrative "My Adventurous Day"_
6. _____
7. _____
8. _____

Good Points About My Writing	Ways to Improve My Writing
I stay focused on the topic.	Add vivid, descriptive adjectives.
My main idea is clear.	Use stronger transition words.
I use details to support topic sentences.	Vary my sentence structure.
I've used correct paragraphing.	Proofread for spelling & punctuation
I have an introduction and conclusion.	

Notes: Use my Thesaurus to help improve my adjectives. "Furthermore" is my new favorite transition word. Others are in my writing folder. When I proofread, I should go backwards so I look at each word.

difficult subject matter of the latter unit. Students will often remark that the government assessment seemed harder than the tall tale assessment. Although this may be true, as some units are inherently more difficult to grasp than others, providing support may be all that's needed to minimize this problem and the lack of fairness students might feel. For example, cautioning students about particular questions or clarifying responses to questions is one way to help level the playing field for instructional units that may be more complex than others. Another method is to adjust the test and/or the grading system to accommodate varying degrees of complexities in any given unit. For example, by adding bonus questions or assigning different point values to questions, students will understand that you have tried to be equitable.

♦ *Discouraging fluctuations: matters of student effort*—Students' progress might waver because their effort is inconsistent. We've often witnessed students' wavering results and recognize that the ability to consistently perform well may be challenging for most students. Allowing some performance parameters seems more feasible for a majority of students whose grades might mildly fluctuate. In our experience, mild wavers between one to three points seemed comfortable. However, if student progress fluctuates more than this, various methods of intervention could be called into action. The teacher could meet with the students to discuss the outcomes and devise action plans. For example, if students are struggling to grasp content despite using their best effort, a plan to include more teacher support as well as student practice can be put into effect. Likewise, if the students are tripped up because of effort—which could be for numerous reasons—plans are put into effect to remove those issues that interfere with the students using their best effort. In essence, we try to build parameters into our monitoring systems that will help us know when and how we can intervene on behalf of our students.

♦ *Levels of frustration*—Some students may grow frustrated by minimal or lack of improvement. Providing teacher support and encouragement may be necessary. As mentioned earlier, some students may not have had much experience accepting responsibility and/or holding themselves accountable on matters. The idea of directing their own improvement by building their skills will itself take some getting used to. Repeated practice and direct instructions may be necessary as students learn to develop and apply their skills. Even students who continuously hover at a near-perfect score may demonstrate levels of frustration. For these students, it may be necessary to create unique systems of encouragement and reward so they are assured their performance is extremely good. Teacher recognition through a brief note, supportive words, or another method may be all that's needed to ward off their feelings of frustration.

- *No need to share results!*—At times students may need reminders that their self-monitoring activities are for their own improvement. No one is expected to share their results with classmates. As some students may be compelled to compare their results with others, stating a "privacy policy" about grades may help you resolve matters like this. You might also find that some students gladly (and loudly) share their results—both good and bad—for attention, praise, or a host of other reasons. Curtailing this through the same classroom policy could help with these issues as well.

- *Rewards*—Determining if rewards are appropriate is a decision best left to you. At times, providing a reward may serve as the impetus to jump start some students into action, while at other times, the effects may be negligible. Some teachers choose to give rewards intermittently, whereas others provide stickers and other forms that align with visual display. Using praise is another option that is effective. Words of praise can be used to recognize accomplishments and/or encourage positive performance.

Other Ideas for Self-Monitoring Within Literacy Activities

- Any type of activity that has enough consistency and/or standardization so students can evaluate their continuous progress using comparable criteria is a good candidate for this technique, such as spelling tests that are administered weekly or biweekly. Even word-processing skills assessments qualify, providing they are given routinely.

- Quarterly assessments, such as benchmarks to determine each student's reading level, is a skill that also works well with monitoring. Encouraging students to demonstrate their improved skill (every quarter) to outperform their previous assessment is one avenue to take.

- Written activities can also be used just as readily as short answer, matching, or other formats. Oftentimes using rubrics that may already be in place is one way of working with these types of activities, especially if students are responsible for writing routinely.

- Any type of pre- and posttest would also work well. Encouraging students to demonstrate their improved skill on a posttest is a challenge most students will eagerly accept.

Wrap-up on Self-Monitoring Devices

What better way to ensure steady progress than by monitoring change over time. Using self-monitoring devices, students not only begin to accept responsibility and accountability for their actions and performance, but they also begin to understand their role in affecting their progress. By witnessing growth while simultaneously identifying areas that need strengthening, students are given the foundation for autonomous learning—the unique path each can follow to support his or her own academic growth.

Common Ideas Among the Superhero Strategies

As mentioned at the onset of this chapter, these strategies are in some way integrated into existing classroom practice or instruction. This is the reason they've been called process strategies; they are part of a larger process. In addition to this important element, there are other critical factors that are shared among them, including the following:

♦ *Visual display*—Many of the strategies include some method of visual display as a means to encourage and reward students. Considering methods to display student work, to promote successful achievement, and to establish expectations (even though they will demonstrate varying degrees of ability and achievement) are child-friendly ways to encourage improved participation, effort, and motivation.

♦ *Student–teacher relationships*—All of the strategies require that teachers encourage and support their students' effort and also remove barriers that interfere with their students' success. Implied in this requirement is the need for teachers to know their students well, including their likes and dislikes, as well as their strengths and weaknesses, and other defining characteristics (such as issues that might interfere with their level of motivation, discussed in Chapter 4). In addition to spending time interacting with their students and reviewing and monitoring student work, teachers glean additional insights about their students by requesting feedback from them on particular issues. (Chapter 4 discusses methods of surveying and obtaining student feedback.) Establishing a good rapport with students is not enough. Being able to help students feel successful and achieve academically is critical.

♦ *Student–teacher expectations*—Although not expressly stated, these activities require top performance and commitment not only from students but from teachers, too. Building a support network of colleagues with whom you can share, shape, and reshape ideas is extremely helpful as you champion the cause of increasing student motivation.

♦ *Teacher intervention and guidance is provided routinely*—Although many of the activities encourage students to work together or independently, the teacher plays an important role in guiding and monitoring all activities. The teacher needs to be available to intervene as necessary. Some students will need more teacher involvement than other students. (Chapter 4 discusses this further.)

♦ *Desired outcomes are clearly established and followed*—Reminders are plentiful. Each strategy incorporates some element of clarifying parameters so that students are clear about expectations, both behavioral and performance-based. Although the importance of establishing these parameters at the onset of an activity is obvious, it's also important to note that adhering to them once they're set is equally critical. Because you may be asking more of your students than what they're used to—whether this has to do with academic expectation or simply ways in which they will be working together with classmates—this may prove challenging. Acknowledging that reminders and reviews are necessary will help you meet this challenge on all fronts.

♦ *Rewards*—Although we remain neutral on the topic of rewards, we do acknowledge that we have placed ourselves in the world and environment of students ranging from the ages of eight to twelve years. Thinking like an eight- to twelve-year-old may be the best way to reach an eight- to twelve-year-old. It's just a thought. Even experts like Annette Breaux and Todd Whitaker assert that the real secret of using rewards is using them effectively. "The value that we as teachers place on the student's actions that lead to the reward is at least as important as the actual reward" (Breaux & Whitaker, 2006, p. 122).

Making Them Your Own

These strategies are flexible and there are countless ways to alter or tweak them so they better align to your unique circumstance and needs. What may work for one teacher may not necessarily work for another. Decisions about which ideas to integrate and how to integrate them are best determined by the teacher. Your unique starting point, your desired outcomes, and your vision all play a role in this process.

Motivation Improvement Tip #4: Determine Which Superhero Strategies Align with Your Plans and Can Best Be Integrated into Your Instructional Processes

There's no time like the present to begin. It's been our experience that discussion with our colleagues of the Superhero strategies is the point at which most begin to feel empowered to initiate the challenge of building student motivation in their classrooms, buildings, and districts. Not only are the strategies concrete and easy to embrace, but they glimmer with hope as they add something new to that which already exists and is familiar; they are very doable and can be incorporated into many types of literacy-based classroom activities and instruction. Now is a good time to begin thinking of how to use them in your classroom, which activities are both appropriate and suitable for you.

Although you might instinctively know which activity or activities you would like to try (we suggest beginning with no more than two), you might first wish to review the work you did in Chapter 1 to create a starting point, establish goals, and articulate a philosophy statement. In addition to reviewing your own plan, you might wish to consider answers to the following guiding questions; your answers might help you decide which strategies will work best for you.

♦ Are there any strategies that seem better aligned with my starting point and my goals (as well as my philosophy)?

- Are there any strategies that seem more likely to work well with my method of instruction (reading instruction or other forms of literacy instruction)?

- In what ways will I need to alter the strategies presented in the examples in this chapter so they'll work well in my classroom?

- Are there any changes I might want to consider making to my instruction to accommodate a Superhero strategy?

- If I don't have the materials I need, can I readily get them? Or can I alter the strategy to make do with the materials I do have?

Once you've considered your responses to these questions and selected one or two Superhero strategies to try out in your classroom, add the ideas to your plan. Remember, they can be changed if you change your mind, they don't work, or for a variety of other reasons. It's critical to allow yourself the freedom to revise your plan.

Figure 2.15 (page 66) is a sample Motivation Improvement Initiative Action Plan that includes sample responses from the earlier Motivation Tips. As all activities in this sample plan centered on writing a research paper, the teacher determined she could introduce the idea of teaming competitions into this process. She felt it aligned with her goals and could also be integrated into the writing process which was used for the Research Paper project. The teacher determined she could use existing writing checklists to award points and could also use the teacher check state in the process to tally the points. Finally, she noted that other collaborators might be needed, such as a support teacher who could provide assistance with writing (a need she identified earlier and now had some better parameters for providing to the collaborator).

The teacher also wished to try a version of a mini book club where students who were grouped together could read brief biographies on the presidents of others in their group. This might enable the students to take a more active role in the writing process as they performed their peer editing. She noted that the librarian might be willing to collaborate on this part of the assignment. She further noted that the technology teacher might also be a good collaborator to help access information about the presidents online. For example, she could provide good websites for students to access.

Figure 2.15. The Motivation Improvement Action Plan Sample with Tip #4

Starting Point: *Improve student performance on third-quarter Presidential Research Paper (and explore overall improvement in writing)*

Goals:
- *Students to apply their beginning research skills (learned and practiced)*
- *Improve writing skills and writing process skills*
- *Produce a quality research paper that demonstrates use of writing process and beginning research skills*

Collaborators: *Librarian and Writing Support Instructor*

Philosophy Statement: *All students will be held accountable for demonstrating use of all skills and strategies which were taught and practiced for writing a research paper (Each according to his/her ability)*

Expression of the Ideal: *Meet with success and develop a belief in the importance of the skill and come to value the process involved.*

Superhero Strategies:

1. *Teaming Competition*

   Ways to Adapt: *Use established "reading" groups for peer editing "writing groups." (Allow some smaller groups as students complete rough drafts). Use writing process checklists as criteria for competition. Award points during teacher check.*

   Collaborators: *AIS Writing Support*

2. *Mini Book Clubs*

   Ways to Adapt: *Locate brief biographical info on presidents. Have a two-day mini book club allowing students working through the writing process together to read and discuss biographies of presidents covered by others in their group.*

   Collaborators: *Librarians for biographies; Computer teacher other access*

3

Underdog
Strategies to the Rescue!

Underdog strategies are those quick fixes that come to the rescue in the nick of time. Or, they present a dashing dose of something new, something extraordinary that grasps the attention of all students. Although extremely useful, these *quick-fix* and *gotcha* strategies may have a very temporary classroom shelf-life.

Books abound that list quick motivational remedies to engage otherwise unengaged students. Some may be linked to well-established classroom management practices, whereas others may be suited to instructional approaches or teaching styles. Supplementing and supporting your motivation improvement initiative by adopting some of these Underdog Strategies can strengthen your collective efforts. Although their effects many not be lasting, they nonetheless tend to be quick, easy-to-use, and temporarily effective. They have a definite place and serve a definite purpose within the larger framework of your improvement plans.

Motivation Improvement: Quick-Fix and Gotcha Strategies

Unlike the Superhero strategies discussed in Chapter 2, these Underdog techniques are not necessarily ones that need to be integrated into your larger classroom routine nor linked to a larger process. Many are simple and smaller in scope than the Superhero strategies and may only be effective for a limited period of time. In addition, many of the Underdog strategies are easy to initiate and can be clustered together and used at the same time. Like the Superhero strategies, they are extremely flexible and will work well with a variety of language arts and literacy activities.

We've selected techniques for inclusion in this chapter that represent the following:

♦ They include fresh ideas and incorporate recent educational practices, technologies, or materials.

♦ They are considered *classics* and have withstood the test of time.

♦ They are flexible and easy to use with literacy activities across the curriculum.

Each technique is described and helpful ideas to integrate them into your classroom are included. Classroom vignettes, as well as teacher and student "voices," that help paint a picture of these strategies in action are included. Also, we've provided cross-references where strategies may overlap. Like Chapter 2 on Superhero strategies, this chapter ends with a brief discussion that spotlights the similarities among all of the Underdog strategies. These shared factors provide insightful glimmers of what makes these Underdog strategies so valuable.

Action... Action... and More Action!

We all know how difficult it is to sit still for long periods of time. We also know that it can be difficult to monitor when students are paying attention and comprehending what's going on in class. This is especially true for literacy activities that involve thinking processes that are "unseen." Allowing students to stay active usually increases their time on task. Having the students interact in the following ways may keep them from drifting away and as well as help the teacher monitor for understanding:

♦ Give a "thumbs up" or "thumbs down" in response to a teacher's prompt.

♦ Devise other hand signals to represent degrees of understanding.

- "Lip" the answers to the teacher.

- Hold up answers.

- Share ideas with a partner.

- Share with the class.

- Compare answers with other group members.

- Move around the classroom.

Does This Happen in Your Classroom?

I wanted to be sure that my students were able to correctly identify the main idea in some short reading comprehension passages we were reading together. As we worked through our multiple-choice questions following each passage, I asked the students to raise their hand and "lip" their answer to me—a, b, c, or d. I would then scan the classroom, and point at the student whose hand was raised, which was that student's cue to "lip" his or her answer to me. I could immediately tell who was getting it, and who needed more help. Plus, I could keep this information discrete and correct misunderstandings immediately.

Mr. Parsons, Third-Grade Teacher

Bonus Incentives

Although controversial, incentives can be very motivating to some students. They can be varied and used as frequently or infrequently as you like. Offering bonus points on a test or extra credit for certain assignments give students the opportunity to challenge themselves. It also helps them assume more control over their own grades. Homework passes can also be a great reward or incentive to students. These types of rewards take little time to prepare and involve no cost.

It is important to ensure that all students have an equitable opportunity to earn extra credit and bonus points. For example, if students must use a computer for research, they should be given the option to use school computers as not all students have home computers.

A Peek into the Classroom

Ms. Chase was famous for her "solve-and-support" extra-credit assignments where she asked students to find answers to questions that came up during class instruction. For example, at the start of her geography unit, her third-grade students were often baffled by Greenland (which most assumed is a continent) and asked numerous questions about it. For one of her solve-and-support assignments, Ms. Chase asked students to find information that would help answer the question, "What's up with Greenland?" Ms. Chase also required that students support their answers by bringing in books, information from websites, and other types of "evidence" that they could share with the class.

Certificate Awards for Achievement

Recognition certificates can be used to congratulate individual effort and performance for any type of literacy activity. Certificates can be purchased or computer generated to be specific to a student's accomplishment.

Considering clever twists to the standard certificate is one way to encourage students to try something new or different. For example, adding symbols or stickers to the certificate may entice some such as by including musical notes on a certificate that recognizes the use of "voice" in a narrative essay. Additional examples include incorporating crossword puzzles on certificates that acknowledge students' use of vocabulary in their writing or speaking activities; using uniquely shaped certificates to spruce up certificates; awarding "light bulb" certificates for outstanding effort on an informational essay on Thomas Edison; and distributing "megaphone" certificates in recognition of great speaking skills. These ideas can be used with a variety of topics and can recognize an assortment of student achievements. Using shape notepads from a teacher specialty store and handwriting the certificate is one way to do this with relative ease.

Presenting the certificate in front of the class or mailing it home can send the message that the achievement was important or special.

Character Education Connections

Many of the character education traits encouraged by most schools are traits that a motivated learner would likely possess, such as responsibility, respectfulness, and perseverance. Students can be involved in the presentation of character education information by researching and disseminating the meaning of the character traits, creating/performing skits for other students, or by writing essays about students who display specific character traits, and more. Encouraging the display of these traits will, in turn, encourage the display of improved class habits, which should positively impact student performance. As further incentive, you may want to keep a permanent list of each student who is a good example of each trait or publish the names of students who are good role models in the school newsletter or local newspaper. Finally a postcard or letter of recognition sent to a child's home can be a great badge of honor, as well as a great motivational example for others.

Choice

Our research shows that a very effective way to improve student motivation is to allow students to have more choices. The opportunities to provide choice in a classroom are vast and often overlooked. Some ideas for use of choice in literacy activities include:

- ♦ Selecting one of two essay questions for an assessment.
- ♦ Completing ten of fifteen multiple-choice questions.
- ♦ Choosing a book, partner, seat, etc.
- ♦ Determining which homework assignment to select.

- Deciding the order in which tasks can be completed (start at the bottom and work up, random, etc.).
- Assisting with activity plans.

These types of choices can be used with numerous literacy activities. Their objective is to give students a feeling of independence and ownership that increases the likelihood that the students stay interested and show their best effort.

Computers and Technology

As computers become more common in homes and classrooms, the programs and websites continue to improve. There are many academic sites that look and function like video games yet have embedded academic value. For example, sites abound that can help students build skills in spelling, grammar, syntax, punctuation and more. Some sites are available through publishers and may require a subscription or supplement a textbook series, whereas others are available for public access.

Over the years we've phased out a few of our lengthy research papers in favor of having our students create slideshow presentations. The students still research topics, take notes, and record information as in the past, only now they're working in a different format. Some of the students who struggle with the process of preparing a research paper move gracefully though similar structures while using the computer slideshow software.

The use of new technologies excites most students and teachers. Some students would love to share their writing or edit their writing under a document camera. The uses of Smart Board technology in the classroom are also endless. For example, we've used the Smart Board to introduce a unit on Tall Tales in which each student was given an opportunity to interact with the technology as the student constructed new meaning about this popular genre. There are also numerous website activities that can be used with this technology. Blogging is another way in which students can communicate and share ideas with one another and with their teacher. We've replaced some of our book discussions and journal writing with blogs so students have the opportunity to chat with others about their ideas. Students access the blogs through their teacher websites; they can share the blog writing with their family members. Students also can use video or webcams to record presentations, practice reading, add video to a slide presentation, and more.

Some students will work hard for the simple benefit of earning computer time. The computer may be used to make daily instruction more motivating, or it may be used as a reward for successful effort or performance.

Does This Happen in Your Classroom?

My students began blogging this year. For their first assignment, I asked them to share which comprehension strategy was their favorite and why. We had just finished reading our first book, and we had practiced using eight strategies. I was shocked at the ideas that they shared in their blogs, which were thoughtful and well supported. I'm not convinced they would have used the same level of effort had they simply been discussing their ideas during class.

Ms. Liang, Fourth-Grade Teacher

Contests

Essay contests, poster contests, spelling bees, and more....Students love a challenge! There are many opportunities to offer students team or independent challenges that appeal to different modalities. We've found that our local newspaper periodically offers holiday-related writing contests, and several popular educator magazines, such as *Storyworks*, have contests relating to book reviews and creative writing. In addition to these popular types of writing contests, there are others that offer unique opportunities and may appeal to some students. For example, historical homesteads or associations may sponsor debates or oratorical competitions where students present speeches about a topic or person or deliver parts of well-known speeches.

Does This Happen in Your Classroom?

Carol Anne was an average student who worked hard to get good grades. As we studied our local history unit, she became fascinated with some of the prominent figures from the past who contributed to the growth of our area. One of the local historical associations was sponsoring a competition, inviting students to recite parts of speeches and letters originally delivered by these well-known figures. Carol Anne jumped at the chance to take part in the event.

Mrs. Watkins, Sixth-Grade Teacher

Class contests, such as a spelling bee or trivia game, could be contained within one classroom, or held schoolwide. Prizes need not always be part of the challenge, as the "glory" of winning is often reward enough.

Although your initial search to identify appropriate contents may take some time, we've found that colleagues and administrators often like to relay contest information once they're aware of your interest in participating in them.

Displays

Many students take great pride in having their work prominently displayed. It's comparable to "hanging on the refrigerator," only on a grander scale. Student work may be displayed in a classroom, hallway, or common area in the school. You may want to create a rotating class display highlighting one student's work. Although student work displays are not novel, they can quickly become the center of attention and charge-up student enthusiasm simply by using a new or unusual term that adds pizzazz, for example:

- Gallery
- Exhibit
- Showcase
- Platform
- Concession
- Chat Board
- Hall of Fame

There are other avenues you might wish to take with displays. You can ask students to share their work with another class or during the school's public announcements. Your school or district may have a newspaper or newsletter in which students can have their work highlighted. Thinking beyond your own school, you may be able to display student work at the public library, community center, nursing home, or other public area. Teachers should carefully monitor work that will be displayed to the public and be careful to offer *all* students the opportunity to have their work shown.

Public displays could also be used to recognize individual achievements. To encourage students to do their best writing, complete writing assignments, or follow the writing process, you could have an "Author of the Month" bulletin board. The selected student or students can display a variety of their writing. Classmates might then be encouraged to ask the honorees questions about how they got their ideas or other information. (*See also* "Goals—Making 'em Stick," page 79, later in this chapter.)

A Peek into the Classroom

Mrs. Taylor knew her students looked forward to having their work displayed at the local library. She took great care in helping each student showcase his or her best work. She knew that focusing on each student's strength might mean that she would be sending some lengthy written assignments, some group projects, and some student-created books. Having a variety made the display interesting. She loved to hear the students report with pride that their families had gone to see their work.

"Do-Overs"

One goal in education is to help students achieve and gain knowledge. When student work is incorrect or off task, simply marking it as such does little to help the student reach that goal. It often leaves the student (and the teacher) feeling like a failure. Our Read-Along Guides (Athans & Devine, 2008) allow students repeat opportunities to practice reading comprehension skills and provide numerous chances to grow with teacher supervision. Applying that same theory to other literacy assignments may increase a student's feeling of success and build the student's overall understanding of a topic. Perhaps clarifying directions, redirecting a response, reviewing a sample, or demonstrating use of a resource may help a student perform better on a second try. This second try or "do-over," sends the message that you believe the student can be successful.

Additionally, a clear message is sent when work that isn't done well needs further effort. This may make some students try harder the first time around. Others may need continued support yet will benefit from the chance to *try again*.

A Peek into the Classroom

Through his hard work and effort, Gordon was finally able to organize his weekly letter home to his parents, a routine assignment through which students share highlights of their week. His introduction was engaging, each paragraph focused on one key idea and contained strong supporting details, and his conclusion was well done. Yet, when he was given an assignment to write a fictitious pen-pal letter for social studies, his letter was disorganized and rambling. Ms. Granger explained to Gordon that the assignment was very similar to the "Friday letter home" assignment. She even showed him how the structure of one of his home letters (which she had copied for her files) could be used for the new assignment. She gave Gordon a "do-over" on the pen-pal assignment and was pleased to see how much better he performed on the second try. Gordon beamed when he received his new grade.

Enthusiasm

As many of these strategies suggest, maintaining your enthusiasm is vital to keeping your students interested. It's important to vary and mix things up. You might want to dress in costume, play the guitar, bring in a guest speaker, incorporate technology, alter assessments, involve families, work in groups, or something else. For example, when our students were studying rocks and minerals in science, we planned a "rock party," playing on the word rock (to possibly mean rock and roll). The students arrived at their party having been instructed to bring their own rock or mineral sample and excitedly wrote lengthy, well-constructed paragraphs describing the physical properties of their sample—which was actually their assessment for the rocks and minerals unit. Our enthusiasm about a potentially uneventful and challenging concept became something all students looked forward to and succeeded with.

Having varied lessons that burst with enthusiastic activities, and emphasize the *thrill* that accompanies the learning will keep students from becoming indifferent. (*See also* "Out-of-the-Ordinary Activities and Ideas," page 82, later in this chapter.)

Food-Centric Incentives

Although using food as an incentive is controversial, we've seen numerous examples of teachers using food in the classroom to support a range of literacy experiences. For example, candy has been used as markers for bingo boards to build content vocabulary, to practice recognizing parts of speech and punctuation, and to revisit common spelling rules. Treats are commonly used to reward individual and class performance for challenging computer activities, compelling writing assignments, or outstanding note-taking and listening activities. Likewise, in many classrooms, a student may select a favorite treat from a candy jar or a class can earn pizza or popcorn for a reward. The practices and possibilities are endless.

Some examples of food-related lessons we use are as follows:

♦ After studying New York State and creating slideshow brochures that involve a range of literacy skills, all six of our fourth-grade classes are involved in the *New York State Cookie Project*, which has become a legendary culminating activity and the buzz of the school. Using a cutout cookie shaped like New York, we have students identify different geographic features and landmarks using blue icing to show bodies of water, chocolate chips to symbolize mountain ranges, small candies to indicate large cities and the state capital, and a special candy to highlight our hometown. A local bakery makes the cookies using a cookie cutter shaped like New York State (which we had specially made by a tinsmith). Parents provide the topping to help us highlight many important features. It is a special project worthy of the attention it creates.

♦ While working within the Colonial time period when families were often responsible for making their own goods, we provide students with step-by-step directions for making butter. Students follow the directions and, providing they haven't skipped steps or misread information, end up enjoying a tasty treat. To add variety and excitement to this activity, we encourage students to choose the jar they wish to use to make their butter. The size of the jar greatly affects how quickly they will complete the steps and adds to the thrill of making their butter.

Food can also be used to encourage a desired behavior, to rally group spirit before a big test, or to celebrate success. Several examples of each are provided below.

♦ Having a group snack or breakfast on the day of a big test or potentially stressful event can help ease anxiety. With the quantity of assessing that's required in most schools today, many students, teachers, and parents can't help but feel concern. Although it's important to be sure students are properly prepared, have had enough rest, and have eaten a nourishing breakfast, a simple snack or a healthy treat shared with the entire class helps to ease the stress. Parents are usually eager to provide the food and are thankful that teachers are aware of the amount of pressure some students feel during assessments.

♦ Similar to the snack or breakfast before a big test, nothing says "phew" like a special treat after the fact. Taking your class outside for an ice cream treat after an especially difficult event may help some students to unwind.

♦ In addition to celebrating your students' successes, another use of food is to celebrate milestones for people, characters, and events that are a part of your curriculum. For example, celebrating Johnny Appleseed's birthday by eating apples is one way to bring to life the contributions of this legendary folk hero, or acting out the first Thanksgiving is another classic food-centric activity.

♦ Participating in family-oriented celebrations, such as Grandparents' Day, helps build school support and send the positive message that school matters. Inviting grandparents to school for tea and cookies is another extension of food celebrations.

A Peek into the Classroom

Mrs. Ashford, a reading specialist, encourages her students to sign out books and other materials for use at home. The benefits of their extra reading and literacy activities are clear. As an incentive for students to return the books in a timely manner, Mrs. Ashford rewards them with a small piece of candy with each return. She even has a specific candy she believes encourages them to return the materials promptly! Using this system, Mrs. Ashford is able to maintain the students' interest in working with materials at home throughout an entire school year.

Incorporating cooking into a lesson is another common activity that uses food as its theme. Cooking with a class can be very motivating and teaches skills that stretch beyond the classroom. To wrap-up a unit of study about a specific geographic region or culture, the students could prepare a meal or food item related to what they have learned. The process of preparing food, as well as trying new food, is a great experience, not to mention the important skill of following directions in a recipe.

Despite the controversy, students seem to be motivated by food or the social interaction involved with eating. Yet it's also important to keep in mind that using food-centric activities sparingly heightens their impact. Also, despite your own feelings about the use of food, it may be necessary for you to review your school's policy on the issue. Some districts discourage the use of certain foods or have restrictions on food preparation.

Games

We have seen many examples of games being used in classrooms as successful motivators for students. "Buzz-in" games using individual controllers, *Jeopardy* Power Point, web-based games, card games, and more are powerful motivators that have recently gained popularity with the new technologies (*see also* "Computers and Technology," page 72, earlier in this chapter). All are hands-on ways to deliver literacy-related instruction through a variety of modalities and many allow teachers to monitor individual participation and effort. Having the opportunity to "team-up" with other students and engage in some friendly competition can also be helpful. Allowing students to earn game days or choice activities may increase their time on task, help review material, and relieve pressure of an already stressful curriculum.

In addition to new computer based games, many students still enjoy the classic standbys such as *Four-Square*, *Seven-Up*, and others. Although these games may not have the same type of instructional appeal as the newer computer games, they nonetheless can be used intermittently to relieve tension or as a culminating activity to reward performance.

Brainstorming with colleagues will enable you to assemble a good repertoire of new and classic games.

Gatherings

Sometimes bringing students together for brief intermittent gatherings will motivate them into action. At times we've assembled a "lunch bunch" where we'll invite from three to five students to join us for lunch in our classrooms. Sometimes we encourage them to share their views about books we're reading, other times we'll ask for their input about special projects or writing activities. Sending the message that their ideas matter boosts their confidence and encourages them to participate.

Grades

Many students take on a new sense of commitment for their work when they feel they have some "say" in the way their work will be graded. Students can be involved in their grading in many ways. Having them help to create and use grading rubrics will clarify an assignment's objectives and enable them to set goals. For example, having them help to design a rubric for oral presentations that incorporates speaking, listening, and note-taking skills is one way to encourage their active participation in all of these literacy activities. Also, helping to devise rubrics for specific projects, such as writing assignments, may encourage them to take a fresh look at desired outcomes that they have overlooked or ignored through complacency. Another idea involving rubrics is to periodically use a "double rubric system" whereby students grade their assignments first and then the teacher provides his or her grades. Discrepancies between student and teacher grades are discussed with the objective of helping students take charge of their improvement.

Students may also be asked to track their grades over time and are always eager to see their results head in a positive direction (also discussed in Chapter 2). This is helpful because the students track their own progress without being compared to others, and they continue to try to surpass their previous grade.

Another helpful idea to encourage a positive grade-consciousness is to show students examples of what constitutes successful performance. This may help clarify assignment objectives. Likewise, modeling how work can be improved is a powerful way to address and strengthen "typical" weaknesses.

Creating a "peer review" system is another option that you may wish to consider when appropriate. Here, students may choose to have a classmate review an assignment to help catch errors before it's turned in for a grade. Calling upon the help of students who demonstrate strong skill in particular areas will improve its effectiveness.

Lastly, having the opportunity to redo assignments or complete extra credit allows a student more control over their own grades (*see also* "Do-Overs," page 74, and "Bonus Incentives," page 70, earlier in this chapter).

Goals—Making 'em Stick!

Encouraging students to display individual or group goals helps them stay focused and in some instances, provide for some helpful peer rallying and friendly competition. A large, centrally located bulletin board also serves as a visual reminder of goals or milestones. Some bulletin board ideas are as follows:

- ◆ Reaching required reading goals (number of books/pages read as a class or individual).
- ◆ Displaying beginning-of-the-year goals.
- ◆ Adding names of students who have reached certain milestones.
- ◆ "Wall of Fame" where students can display work they believe shows their best effort.
- ◆ Display of collaborative or group projects.

Each classroom may have a bulletin board to show individual or group accomplishments, or the entire school may work together on a group display. As each student in a school completes reading a book, they may add a paper book with their name on it to a schoolwide display. The goal may be to have paper books wrap around the school building. A more competitive suggestion might be for each classroom to display paper books to determine which class reaches the preset goal first. The central location and high visibility will keep the topic or goal a priority and can show parents and other visitors what is going on at your school. (*See also* "Displays," page 73, earlier in this chapter.) Figure 3.1 is a photograph of a visual display.

Figure 3.1. Goal Display

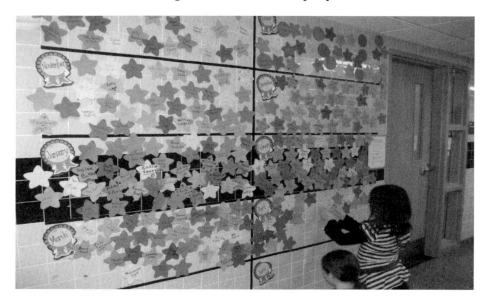

Does This Happen in Your Classroom?

I have my middle school students set three goals at the beginning of each school year. We hang them on the back wall and periodically revisit them. Having this display reminds them of what they were going to try to work on this year.

Ms. K., Sixth-Grade Teacher

Group Privileges

Students often work independently to improve their own grades. Yet, there are times when encouraging a group to work together will benefit the class. Creating a classroom environment that is positive and conducive to learning can be a group goal. Likewise, meeting class reading goals is something that students can encourage each other to do. An example of a group goal may be putting a marble in a jar whenever the teacher sees an example of a student encouraging another student, or each time a book is recorded on a class reading list. When the jar is full, the class earns the predetermined incentive. Group rewards can be, for example, lunch in the classroom, a party, a special game or movie, extra free-time, extra computer time, or a field trip. Keep in mind that the size of the jar and the criteria for earning a marble will determine how frequently the class earns the reward, factors that the teacher can easily control.

Does This Happen in Your Classroom?

I kept a clear jar on my desk so all of my students could see it. They could also keep track of the number of marbles it held. At the beginning of the school year we decided how we, as an entire class, could "earn" a marble for the jar. Some of our criteria included whenever we worked well during a guided-reading activity or if we all met an academic goal, such as performing well on our spelling activities. Each time the jar became full, the class earned a pizza party, an award they decided in advance. The marble jar motivated everyone.

Mrs. McGregory, Third-Grade Teacher

Home Contact

Some teachers may only contact students' homes when there is a problem. Likewise, districts often require formal reporting systems to parents, such as report cards and interim reports. Why not look for opportunities to contact your students' homes to report achievements or other good news? Some examples of times to contact students' homes are when students:

♦ Grasp concepts that have proved difficult for them.

♦ Improve challenging behaviors.

♦ Reflect a positive attitude.

- Use great vocabulary in a writing assignment.

- Select books that are different from their usual—perhaps a new genre, unfamiliar content, or a different format such as a graphic novel.

- Participate well in discussions with classmates.

- Write engaging assignments about family events.

- Share insightful ideas in oral presentations.

- Master new or intricate computer techniques.

Our school provides all students with an assignment notebook. Many teachers use these as a mode not only to record assignments but also to pass on congratulations and brief news about a student's success. A quick note about a child's great attitude or improved effort means a lot to a parent. Mailing a special postcard or jotting a note on a special piece of stationary can be equally impressive. Students are proud to have their progress recognized and shared with their families. Many of these accomplishments may be overlooked by the constraints of many report cards, so parents and students will appreciate the extra time and effort you take to contact them.

Does This Happen in Your Classroom?

Kent's school records showed he struggled with his writing for years. As we began our unit on narrative writing, it was no surprise that he claimed he didn't know what to write. After brainstorming with Kent, I was able to draw from him that he had some unique adventures with his dad who was a long-distance hauler. I encouraged Kent to share a story about his summer travels with his dad and helped him complete his prewriting organizer. His story was very good, and I sent it home to his parents with a note commenting on Kent's success. The encouragement he received from home gave Kent a new outlook on an old problem.

Ms. Washington, Fifth-Grade Teacher

Memory Maps and Other Subtle Reminders

Sometimes a student may need reminders about behavioral expectations they're working toward improving. To help them build their independence and self-monitoring skills, we work with a tool we call a *Memory Map*. Memory Maps are small visual reminders created by a student that feature pictures of the behaviors that student wishes to improve. For example, a student might draw a picture of an assignment notebook as a way to remember to bring it home every night. A picture of a stick figure with a hand raised might be used to remind a student to raise his or her hand instead of calling out. Students come up with their own symbols, create their own map, and determine if they want to tape their map to their desk or place it in a more private area, such as inside a notebook. Some students create their maps after discussing behaviors with their teacher, whereas others create them on their own. The maps simply provide visual reminders that seem to benefit some students. Turning in assignments, bringing materials home, chatting with a neighbor during free-time only, and music lessons after lunch are the kinds of reminders students may chose to represent on their Memory Map, which is often the size of a 3×5-inch card. Taking charge of their improvement can be motivating and fun. Figure 3.2 illustrates an enlarged Memory Map to remind a student of responsibilities such as attending music lessons or being prepared for Physical Education and Library class.

Money System

Classroom currency is motivating and educational. Students earn classroom dollars for a variety of predetermined reasons. This play money can be used to "purchase" homework passes, admission to special events, school supplies, or any award the teacher deems appropriate. The teacher may even charge money for misdeeds, such as not completing a homework assignment. Students can record their earnings in a bank-like ledger. As with many of these reward systems, the teacher can determine how easy or difficult it is for the students to earn money. We've found that if the students are fairly motivated to earn money, then it's beneficial to set goals that make it easy for them to do so. Because there is relatively little expense involved, and it is likely that the goal is for all students to succeed, it makes sense to set attainable goals with this system.

Out-of-the-Ordinary Activities and Ideas

Capture your students' attention by having them use materials that are less common (or sometimes off limits). Holding class outside, in the cafeteria, or library may be an interesting change for students. Allowing students to sit on the floor, in a beanbag chair, or any other atypical location can also be fun. Materials such as a laser pointer, a Smart Board, small dry-erase boards, or even sitting in the teacher's chair are other fun changes that are easy to implement in most classrooms. We have seen teachers dress in character for certain themes, or simply wear a lab coat, hat, or funny glasses to set the mood and captivate their students. Also, you might want to use a little comedy to encourage students, such as by creating classroom book bins that are organized by non-traditional topics: Books About Dogs that Don't Die; Stories About Kids Who Outsmart Their Parents; and the like. Likewise, nontraditional writing assignments may have the same impact, such as "The Top Three Things I Never Want to Do Over Vacation." We realize that some students need the structure of a set routine, but in general, most students will be motivated and interested in varied, hands-on lessons.

In addition to these types of activities, holding special events can entice student interest. Hosting a "Poetry Reception," where students share an original poem, may encourage best-effort work from students. Holding debates, performing Reader's Theater plays or skits, and hosting "open mike" readings are ways to "make mountains out of mole hills" and turn the ordinary into *extraordinary* to encourage student interest and participation. (*See also* "Enthusiasm," page 75, earlier in this chapter.)

Figure 3.2. Memory Map

George's Memory Map

(Violin on Mondays)(9:00lessons)

(Bring-in Library Books from
Home on Wednesdays)

 +

(Sneakers & Basketball for
Phys. Ed. Fridays)

A Peek into the Classroom

To culminate their study of local history, the fourth-grade classes participated in a Local History Showcase where students were able to show off their research papers and displays on their local history projects. Students selected their topics, which included local historical sites, historical events, influential personalities, transportation, area industry, family and home histories, local cemeteries, and more. Teachers provided students with some materials and the village historian supplied copies of original documents for use in students' reports and displays. To help students with their research, the teachers also arranged a bus-tour field trip where they acted as tour guides and discussed historical highlights of the area. The Local History Showcase was held in the cafeteria at the end of the school day. Parents, village officials, and community members were invited to attend. Students shared their work with guests and then viewed projects prepared by their classmates. Although the Local History Showcase took some careful planning, it was a great motivator for students.

Praise That's Pithy and Precise!

Don't underestimate the value of verbal praise. Be generous and be specific. Rather than a simple "Good job!," it's helpful to identify exactly what you think was well done; for example, "I really like how you used voice in your writing" or "I can see how much effort you put into choosing the best vocabulary." Your students will appreciate that you noticed their extra effort, and they will be clear about your expectations. The same thought applies to written praise. When commenting on a student's work, although you can be brief, your comment should still be specific, such as "Great conclusion!" or "Fantastic effort with your handwriting!" Even written symbols can clearly express praise.

Does This Happen in Your Classroom?

I often use a smiley face when a student uses good details to support their main idea. If they don't see a smiley face, they know their details can use some improvement. Conveying information quickly and concisely through this system motivates some of my struggling writers.

Mr. Harrington, Writing Specialist

Scrapbooks

A fifth-grade colleague showed us scrapbooks that her students had created. They were comprised of content-related writing assignments, poetry, and art projects, including student-selected and required work. Some pages were yellowed, with burned edges to mimic age, whereas others were decorated with colorful embellishments and stickers. Keeping a supply of colored paper and stickers for the students to use is necessary, but the focus must remain on showcasing high-quality work. Being allowed to organize and embellish their scrapbook allows students to exercise choice, ownership, and show off their own style. They are eager to share their books with classmates, parents, and other class visitors.

Stickers

Many students respond well to earning a simple sticker reward. It's a basic, inexpensive measure that is nonetheless meaningful for some students. Whether working to fill an incentive chart or as an added bit of encouragement on an assignment, often students look forward to earning this extra praise. Also, a sticker chart tends to be more exact than some other types of visual record-keeping incentives, as the quantity of stickers on a chart is clearly evident. We've used sticker charts to monitor academic goals and to encourage positive behaviors. Letting the students select their own sticker or using stickers that relate to a specific theme may also enhance the impact. Similar to the marble jar, a class sticker chart can be used to track preset objectives so as to earn a certain outcome.

Students in Control

A student, or group of students, can plan a lesson by becoming an "expert" on a topic and teaching what they have learned to the rest of the class. Similar to the commonly known "Jigsaw" model, this can be very basic, such as each person reading a portion of text and summarizing for the class. It could also be more complex, such as having the students plan a formal hands-on lesson of instruction. Students can also be involved in the planning or direction of class activities. Asking questions such as "Would you rather watch a podcast and answer question on a subject, or read a news article and report back to the class?" allows them to take some control. Seeking the students' input as to what they have liked and deemed useful from past lessons can help a teacher plan lessons best suited to the students' interest. Students may also brainstorm lessons or activities that they would like to do in class.

Wrap-up on the Underdog Strategies

Certainly there are numerous other strategies that could qualify as "Underdogs," strategies that can easily be used. Sharing ideas with colleagues, staying current on new information appearing in educational books and magazines, attending conferences, and participating in teacher training courses (if this option is available to you) are ways you can continue to build your resources.

Common Ideas among the Underdog Techniques

The Underdogs are effective as quick-fix and gotcha techniques; their success doesn't rely on their integration into a larger process, their ability to become routine, or even the consistency with which they are used. In addition, there are other critical factors that are shared among them, including the following:

♦ *Wow power*—They provide novelty and are packed with enthusiasm.

- *Student-valued outcome*—Students actively help create, choose, or in some way impact the outcome of many of the strategies. This involvement helps generate student "buy-in."

- *Outcome is viewed as equivalent to the demands of the task*—The strategies help encourage each student to perform to his or her ability, whether working independently or as part of a group. Expectations are realistic and the rewards and recognition are appropriate.

Making Them Your Own

Like the Superhero strategies described in Chapter 2, Underdog strategies can be reshaped to suit your needs within your classroom. Likewise, you might believe that some techniques better align with your teaching style or are better suited to the needs of your students. Having a varied and diverse collection available can be helpful, especially as your needs may change from year to year or even from the beginning of one academic year to the end of that year. Because these techniques might not have lasting appeal (some might only be effective once), having a plentiful selection from which to pick and choose will be useful.

Motivation Improvement Tip #6: Determine Which Underdog Techniques Align with Your Plans, Pique Your Interest, and Seem Suited for Your Classroom Needs and Your Instructional Style and Beliefs

We have found that many teachers already have several favorite techniques that, year after year, continue to grasp their students' attention. If this is the case, one way to begin refining and expanding your collection of techniques is through a self-reflective exercise we've used in our workshops that parallels the *What's on Your Plate* (page 21) activity discussed in Chapter 1. Here we ask participants to list (on a brown paper bag) techniques they've used throughout their teaching career that they believe are "In the Bag" or that have been successful in motivating and engaging their students. Included in this list can also be activities that helped to contribute to outstanding lessons.

Figure 3.3 shows examples from an *In the Bag* activity that could have been noted by the teacher in our sample who is initiating improvement in her Research Paper assignment. On your plan, you might wish to begin by listing your top five strategies and then add to those five additional strategies you would like to try from those described in this chapter. Many of these are easy to integrate into your classroom instruction and activities with little, if any changes needed.

Figure 3.3. Sample In the Bag Activity for Motivation Improvement Action Plan

- Using humor, for example, knock-knock jokes, to review social studies facts

- Awarding stickers that align with the themes of our instruction

- Free "visiting time" with friends

- Inviting students to have lunch in the classroom

- Awarding a homework pass

- Selecting students to be "first" on the lunch line

- Reading chair privileges

- Special treats—healthy snacks

Figure 3.4, page 88, features the Motivation Improvement Action Plan Sample with Tip #6 in place.

Figure 3.4. Motivation Improvement Action Plan Sample with Tip #6

Underdog Strategies	
My Successful Strategies	**Those Strategies I'd Like to Try**
1. Additional computer time	1. Goal setting display board
2. Homework pass	2. New technology use – digital camera
3. Special treats	3. Group snack
4. First in lunch line	4. Friday games
5. Reading chair privileges	5. "Do-overs"

Strategies for the Highly Unmotivated—General Planning for One to Two Students

Targeted Behaviors: _____   Targeted Behaviors: _____
_____   _____
_____   _____

Strategies: _____   Strategies: _____
_____   _____
_____   _____

Interests: _____   Interests: _____
_____   _____
_____   _____

Notes: _____
_____
_____
_____
_____
_____
_____
_____

Reaching the
Highly Unmotivated

Reaching this group of students may take a significant investment of time and commitment. Their disengagement may be pervasive and affect their academics as well as their social relationships with adults, family, and peers. Some new strategies may be helpful.

A wise teaching colleague once commented, "If things don't change, they will always remain the same." Although the simplicity of this fortune-cookie philosophy seems innocent and unalarming, it quickly turns haunting when you think of it in terms of those pervasively unmotivated students whose best hope for change may be initiated by you.

Pervasive Problems

Our original research (Athans, Clarke, Devine, & Sammon, 2005) demonstrated that most students could succeed with our strategy-based reading comprehension approach, as discussed in Chapter 1. We also determined that many of the students who were less successful were challenged by an absence of motivation and effort—the learning process was ineffective when these components were not in place. We then introduced many of the strategies discussed in Chapters 2 and 3 and were able to successfully engage many students. However, a smaller group of students remained unaffected by those strategies. The overriding characteristic that these students shared was the pervasiveness of their difficulty; their lack of motivation affected all content areas and was also evident in their social relationships with adults, family members, and peers. Other characteristics of these students included the following:

- Their academic struggles were documented in school records such as report cards, teacher notes, and/or parent correspondences over the course of one to three years.

- Family matters influenced their academic performance daily and often infringed on their academic responsibilities. For example, some students were excessively absent, others claimed to have numerous home responsibilities that interfered with their ability to complete homework, still others couldn't set aside family problems to accomplish class work both inside and outside of school.

- Many were disinterested in or had difficulty establishing friendships at school.

- Many also had trouble with areas that supported their academic achievement, such as an inability to organize and keep track of materials, work independently, and self-monitor their level of attentiveness and participation.

- School didn't seem to matter.

In addition to the strategies discussed in earlier chapters, it was clear that others were needed to address the needs of these students. Although their struggles spanned across the content areas, we still maintained a strong focus on literacy activities. It was apparent that their lack of engagement in reading and writing activities remained the root of their academic challenges. Yet, we also needed to incorporate some broader remedies to target their unique symptoms. New strategies discussed in this chapter include the following:

- ♦ Discussions with teachers, parents, others
- ♦ Student-Guided Plans
- ♦ Student Contracts
- ♦ Tailored motivational incentives
- ♦ Tailored consequences
- ♦ Mentorship programs

In many ways, these strategies work together like the pieces of a chain that can be linked in a number of different ways. For example, Student-Guided Plans may also rely on the use of Student Contracts. Likewise, a Mentorship might be the result of a Tailored Motivational Incentive. Using these strategies separately or linked with others depends on your unique situation. They are flexible and, like the other strategies, can be adapted as needed. In some cases, they can be used with students who don't demonstrate severe motivational issues. In addition, they could be considered among the Superhero strategies. However, they have been included here because of their effectiveness at helping students who struggle with severe motivational issues or who may be considered at risk unless some type of change is initiated. In all cases, we specify when and how the strategies can be used to help students with varying degrees of difficulty. It's important to keep in mind that some of the discussions and examples in this chapter extend beyond literacy-centered activities. This is a reflection of the pervasiveness of some motivational difficulties.

As in Chapter 2, we describe the techniques and provide glimpses of what they may look like through classroom vignettes. We also highlight some "Solutions to Keep in Mind," which are helpful tips to overcome challenges you might encounter while using them. In these discussions, it becomes clear how these strategies can be used together to help support and encourage students. Lastly, the chapter ends with some brief highlights of the few commonalities among the strategies.

Discussions with Teachers, Parents, School Professionals

It goes without saying that some of your best resources for helping the student who has pervasive motivation issues are the student's parents and other teachers and school professionals/administrators who have some history with the student. Having an informal sit-down discussion with them might give you new insights that wouldn't be apparent in e-mail communications nor from your review of the student's records. However, we aren't suggesting that you base your decisions about a student solely on the recommendations of these sources. Instead, these initial discussions may give you ideas as you create a new starting point for helping the student. Another useful purpose of these meetings is that they may expose some strategies that *haven't* been effective. It is a worthwhile endeavor to explore the past, tryout what may have been successful, and then have other ideas ready as you need them.

A Peek into the Classroom

Whenever Ms. Holliday reviewed her students' portfolios or academic records, she always did so with a healthy dose of skepticism. She knew that students could change a lot from year to year. They could mature, their family situations could be altered, and a variety of other factors could bring about change. She liked to remain objective and not form opinions based on a student's behavior or performance in the past. But about a month into the new school year, Adam continued to show negative attitude, indifference to his school work, and an inability to "fit in" with his fourth-grade classmates—all behaviors that aligned with comments reflected in his past year's report card comments. Ms. Holliday considered a month to be a reasonable amount of "transitional time," so she decided to delve beyond his records and talk with his last-year teacher, Ms. Chou. She learned toward the end of the school year that Adam would check in daily with the art teacher, Mr. B., each morning as he walked to his homeroom. They'd spend just a couple minutes talking about anything, for example, homework or sports. Although the impact on Adam's classroom behavior was small, the relationship he had with Mr. B. was something that Adam sought out and seemed to enjoy. Ms. Chou said that she had been working on developing other positive outcomes using the relationship. For example, she and Mr. B. agreed that Adam could spend some of his recess time in the art room working with Mr. B. and his fifth-grade class, providing he completed his reading assignments. However, there wasn't much time left in the school year to determine the impact. This year Adam's path to his homeroom didn't take him past the art room so his only encounter with Mr. B. was in an art class with 20 other students. Ms. Holliday considered the possibility of trying to reestablish this relationship as a starting point to help Adam.

Solutions to Keep in Mind

♦ *Don't expect the proverbial "magic pill" solution*—During your discussion with others, the chances of finding the perfect solution is slim. In our experience, students who exhibit highly unmotivated characteristics have developed them over a long period of time. Changing them will also take time, and believing that a quick-fix solution will have any permanence is unrealistic. Making small, effective steps toward improvement is a more realistic mind-set to have.

♦ *For transfer students, contact teachers in the districts from which they came*—Should a student transfer into your district, don't hesitate to contact the student's former teachers. Their insights will supplement information from school records and you might also pickup on some classroom management practices that could help support your struggling student. Although some matters may be confidential, those that are not could prove helpful. Samples of the student's reading or writing assignments or other activities may also be valuable.

♦ *Develop partnerships with parents*—Most likely the parent(s) or caregivers of students who struggle with motivation are already aware of the trouble. You might begin by letting them know that your discussion with them is to learn more about their child—what works and what doesn't work—so you can create a plan with them. Involving them in a positive improvement plan could help you win their support. It could also renew their sense of encouragement. If some parents are not aware of their child's difficulties, if they minimize the troubles, and/or if they blame their child's difficulties on others, initiating a starting point with them will be necessary. Sharing a variety of their child's reading, writing, and other assignments with them could help establish a mutual understanding of the kinds of difficulties their child is having. State and district expectations and rubrics may also help to further clarify this.

Student-Guided Plans

We may never fully understand why a student is disengaged, lacks motivation, or is unwilling to apply effort. We can and should attempt to learn as much as possible about our students, yet we may never know the reasons. Still there are things we can do to try and address the behaviors and symptoms that may need changing.

One method we've found effective for some students is the Student-Guided Plan. In the simplest sense, a Student-Guided Plan documents expected actions or behaviors you and your student agree are often absent from the student's typical performance; they're the missing components that result in a student's inability to be successful. Plans are tailored to the student, although the format and monitoring system may be generic. Although we originally called these "checklists," the idea that you and your student have a *plan* of improvement suggests a more positive approach to change. Also, having a plan instead of a checklist places the student at the center of responsibility and distances the role of the "teacher-checker" or "parent-checker." Ultimately, having the student work toward independent self-monitoring is ideal; it is the first step in owning and internalizing the positive behavior. Beginning this complicated and lengthy process with a *plan* seems the best way to start.

Common Characteristics of the Student-Guided Plans

All Student-Guided Plans have the following characteristics in common:

♦ Tasks can be broken down into small, discrete units.

♦ Positive behaviors are identified (either directly on the Plan or through teacher notes).

♦ An incentive system is in place—either in rewards, privileges, or recognition.

♦ Success is achievable, even in small steps.

♦ A simple system of monitoring is in place and parents or others are often involved.

♦ Small inconsequential or insurmountable barriers that threaten progress are quickly identified and replaced swiftly with alternative solutions.

Models of Plans

Figures 4.1 through 4.5 are examples of Student-Guided Plans. A detailed discussion of each follows. Many of the plans focus on a student's literacy-based difficulties; yet, others that are broader in scope have also been included. Again, this is because of the pervasiveness of these students' academic troubles. Each Plan addresses targeted problems and is used for the duration of a specific assignment or longer. Each Plan is very flexible and can be adjusted to address a variety of motivational-related difficulties. Likewise, each Plan may be used with many different literacy-centered activities or broadened as needed.

The student using the Plan in Figure 4.1 (page 96) struggled with his guided-reading assignments. He rarely completed his independent reading activities, or he completed them with minimal effort. This resulted in his inability to effectively participate in his small-group instruction; he gained little benefit from the teacher's targeted instruction, and he grasped little from the ideas contributed by his peers. He worked with his teacher to create a Daily Plan that could be used to span the eight-day instructional unit on Native Americans (a language arts reading unit that coincided with the social studies curriculum). The Plan addressed the issues that prevented him from succeeding:

Figure 4.1. Student-Guided Plan for Daily Reading Activities

Name: _____ Tyler S. _____

Title: _____ If You Lived with the Iroquois by Ellen Levine _____

The following activities were covered or assigned during our Guided Reading instruction today
(check = completed; no check = still to completed)

Date: _____ November 12 _____   Overall Effort: _____ 3 _____

Reading Assignments & Activities	Comment
X Reading p. 18, 19, 20 X Record Main Ideas for each page	You did a nice job recording the main ideas, especially for page 19 — your idea was really clear and well written. Great!
Written Response	Comment
X One response for pgs. 18 – 20	You have some nice ideas in your response. Remember to include details to support your good thinking.
Vocabulary	Comment
X p. 18 extension p. 25 descended p. 19 aisle	Be sure to include the strategies you've used to figure out the word. That way I can see what how you're building your good skills.
Other	Comment
X My work is complete. When you've completed these activities, you can work in the Literacy Bins.	The quality of your work is good. I'm glad you're using your best effort on your reading and then enjoying the Literacy Bins! Excellent!

Comments: I'm thrilled that you're able to stay on track. Great job!

Daily Plan – Guided Reading

The following activities were covered or assigned during our Guided Reading instruction today
(check = completed; no check = still to completed)

Date: _____ November 13 _____   Overall Effort: _____ 3 _____

Reading Assignments & Activities	Comment
X Reading p. 28, 29, 33 X Record Main Ideas for each page	Nice job! I can tell you're carefully selecting your main ideas carefully.
Written Response	Comment
X One response for pgs. 28 – 29 & 33	I enjoyed your response, but I'd like to learn more about your thoughts. Explaining why you think their fishing methods were good would help me.
Vocabulary	Comment
X p. 28 festivals p. 29 utensils p. 33 tanned	Good job with the definitions, especially "tanned" which sometimes confuses students!
Other	Comment
X My work is complete. When you've completed these activities, you can work in the Literacy Bins.	Nice Job, Tyler!

Comments: Excellent job, Tyler. You earned a sticker each day, and that special book you want to borrow is within your reach! Keep going strong!

- Although most students could grasp the routine of the assignments (which appeared on the white board and were reviewed verbally by the teacher at the start of the instructional reading time), this student benefited from having assignments broken down into small, discrete tasks: Reading Assignments and Activities; Written Response; Vocabulary; and Other responsibilities. He also benefitted from teacher comments.

- Where most students could independently monitor their completion of the assignments, this student benefited from more guidance and was provided with a system where he could "check" the tasks once they were completed.

- The student was also asked to monitor his level of effort and rate it using a numeric scale, 1 to 4, so he would become aware that the quality of his work mattered, and that he could make improvements.

- This student was given several incentives. He was awarded a sticker when he completed each daily plan, an incentive he chose. Also, he was rewarded if he could maintain his performance halfway through the instructional unit (completing four Daily Plans) by borrowing a special book from the teacher, another incentive he chose. He received another reward at the conclusion of the instructional unit (completing all eight Daily Plans) where he and his parents worked out an incentive they could offer at home—a family movie night. The student, teacher, and parent worked together to establish the incentive system.

This Plan was stapled to the inside of the student's reading folder. His teacher worked with him daily to help him record the tasks from the white board, although he was encouraged to do this independently by the end of the unit. Whenever he was unable to complete tasks during instructional time, he was responsible for completing them at other times during the school day or as homework. His parents were aware of his Plan and agreed to sign the Plan whenever it needed to come home for completion. This Plan can be used for a variety of routine reading activities.

The Student-Guided Plan shown in Figure 4.2 (page 98) was used with a student who struggled with lengthier writing tasks, whether they were in a content area such as social studies or within language arts. Whereas most students were able to complete a multiple-paragraph assignment in just over an hour (the teacher had provided instruction and practiced the skill over the course of several weeks), this student did not progress at the same rate. Also, she did not demonstrate proficiency with the skills necessary to succeed with the task. Her attention issues also interfered with her progress.

Figure 4.2. Student-Guided Plan for Writing Assignments

Name: _____Crystal J._____ Date: ___1/15 – 1/17___ | Effort: ___3+___
Guided Plan for Writing: _____Colonial Assessment_____ | Time: ___2 hrs___
Assignment: _____'Would You Like to Live in Colonial Times?' Essay_____

__X__ **Read/Restate Task**	Time: __9:00 – 9:15__ Date: __1/15__	
__X__ **Planning** • Bullets/🗝 Words • Bullets/🗝 Words • Bullets/🗝 Words	Time: __9:00 – 9:15__ Date: __1/16__ Good job with your planning, Crystal! Your ideas are focused and you remembered to use key words from the task in your topic sentences. Bravo!	
Break ☺		
Writing __X__ **Intro/🗝 Words**	Time: __9:30 – 9:45__ Date: __1/16__ Let's express your idea in two sentences while keeping your focus general.	
__X__ P { **T** Hard work **1.** Kids had chores **2.** Woke up at sunrise **3.** Bed time was sun set **C** Hard work – no rewards	Time: __9:45 – 10:15__ Date: __1/16__ Your good ideas are well developed! Your closing sentence wrap-up nicely!	
Break ☺		
__X__ P { **T** Not enough fun things **1.** Games seemed unexciting **2.** No team sports **3.** No technology **C** I might not have fun	Time: __9:00 – 9:15__ Date: __1/17__ I like how you described your favorite activities. I could tell you'd miss your sports and your computer games if you lived in Colonial times.	
Break ☺		
__X__ P { **T** Only a few kinds of food **1.** Making meals took time **2.** I'd miss my favorites **3.** Desserts were simple **C** I like today's meals	Time: __9:20 – 9:35__ Date: __1/17__ I like how you described you favorite foods. Nice vivid word choice!	
__X__ **Conclusion//Intro**	Time: __9:35 – 9:50__ Date: __1/17__ I like your conclusion!	

KEY: Bullets/🗝 Words = address all tasks using key words; T = topic sentence; 1, 2, 3 = details; C = conclusion

Having recognized these difficulties early on, the teacher had been providing writing remediation using a popular methodology that used a color-coding scheme to reinforce writing structures. The reading specialist was also involved in supporting the instruction. Although the student was making good gains with her grasp of organizational structures, she struggled applying her learned skill independently; she relied on her teacher's support, and she expressed reluctance to move beyond her color-coded writing papers which, although effective, were becoming time-consuming distractions. As a result of these two factors, she was often able to complete only one out of every three written assignments. It seemed appropriate to continue encouraging her so she could move closer to performing at grade-level expectations.

Her Plan addressed a specific written task and was kept inside her writing folder. As is evident in Figure 4.2, the task is based on a writing assignment included as a part of an end-unit assessment on the Colonial Period, a language arts unit that coincided with social studies. This Plan also breaks down the components into discrete writing functions:

- Read/Restate the task, Planning, and Writing. There is also a further breakdown within each function that makes use of reminders of her teacher's instruction. As an example, her "Planning" will show how she plans to address each part of the task (multiple parts of tasks are often described using bullets) and that she remembers to use *key words* from the task. Also, her "Writing" will be a five-paragraph essay. This includes a two-sentence introduction that uses key words from the task and a two-sentence conclusion that is linked to the introduction. Each paragraph will include a topic sentence (T), roughly three details (1, 2, 3), and a closing sentence (C). Again, these prompts are reminders that incorporate terms and strategies that her teacher uses in daily instruction. Although this may seem very formulaic, it serves as a framework from which she can readily stray once the basics are comfortably in place.

- This Plan also incorporates visual prompts and breaks, both strategies having proven helpful for this student.

- A method to encourage this student to monitor her attentiveness is also included. She was asked to track the amount of time it took her to complete a component and then to note the number of days the assignment required for completion. This monitoring was initially done by the teacher but eventually became the student's responsibility.

- This student was asked to evaluate her effort so she would assume responsibility for improvement. Teacher comments provided encouragement.

- Incentives for this student were built into her breaks. For example, during one of her breaks she could leave the classroom to retrieve the teacher's mail from the school office. For others, she could remain in the classroom and unobtrusively stretch, get a drink, share her progress with her teacher, or simply rest for a few moments at her desk. All were incentives she and her teacher agreed upon in advance.

This type of plan can be used with numerous writing tasks within language arts activities or for other curriculum areas such as social studies. Yet, it must be highly targeted to a specific student's needs and incorporate teaching methods that are in place in the classroom.

Figure 4.3 is a Plan that may work best when used with lengthier projects that incorporate literacy activities. For example, the project featured in this plan was used for a social studies class in which each student was responsible for creating a slideshow presentation about New York State. As the task was already broken down extensively for all students, the teacher used a separate attachment Plan to help this student who struggled with academic and behavioral issues. The student was responsible for monitoring his academic progress, which he did together with his teacher, but special features of this plan included:

♦ A section that addresses his ability to work with others. Because students were responsible for working in small groups during the note-taking component of their preparation, this student's Plan included a section that addressed this behavioral component, reinforcing that he was held accountable for his behavior, a matter that he, his teacher, and the school counselor had been working on improving.

♦ Another difference in this Plan is that the incentive structure is delivered at home. Here, the parents have devised a system based on their child's interest.

Figure 4.3. Student-Guided Plan for Projects with Literacy Activities

Name _____ Sam P _____ Plan Date: _____ February 18 _____

Type of Project: _Slideshow Presentation – State Brochure_ Start Date: _2/18_ End Date: _3/10_

Activity	Plans & Estimated Date to Complete	Ability to Work Well With Others or Independently	Parent/Teacher Check	
Assignment & Grading Rubric Review	Sam & Ms. J. to read assignment & rubric together. 2/19	Sam participated well, carefully reading the assignment & highlighting ideas.	Ms. J. 2/19 Bill P. 2/20	
Research & Note-Taking	Sam to work with Ms. J. & independently during class instruction. 2/20	Nice job today!	Ms. J. 2/20 Bill P. 2/20	
Research & Note-Taking	Library instruction. Sam to work with Mrs. G. and seek help as needed. 2/23	Sam had some trouble working quietly in the library. Mrs. G. reminded him of our Plan.	Ms. J. 2/23 Bill P. 2/24	
Research & Note-Taking*	Sam to work independently during class instruction. 2/25	Great job after getting off to a slow start. Nice progress after getting on track!	Ms. J. 2/25 Bill P. 2/25	**1**
Create Slideshow Storyboard	Sam to work with Ms. J. during computer instruction. 2/27			
Add Text to Slides & Proofread	Library Instruction in Technology Lab. 3/2			
Add Text to Slides & Proofread	Classroom Instruction in Technology Lab. 3/3			
Add Text to Slides & Proofread*	Classroom Instruction in Technology Lab. 3/4			**2**
Research & Add Art	Classroom Instruction 3/6			
Research & Add Art	Classroom Instruction 3/9			
Review Slideshow*	Classroom Instruction 3/10			**3**

Incentives _____ Following Sam's successful completion of activities that are starred, he gains

_____ 1) ½ hour of weekend computer time; 2) a special popcorn & movie night out with Dad;

_____ 3) a family sledding weekend.

As mentioned earlier, the Plans shown in Figures 4.1 (page 96), 4.2 (page 98), and 4.3 (page 101) focus on literacy-based activities, yet other Student-Guided Plans can be used for students who struggle with routine academic issues, such as completing homework, organizational troubles, and lack of effort, in all subject areas. Targeted behavioral issues can also be incorporated in these broad-based plans.

Figures 4.4 and 4.5 (page 104) feature two versions of a plan that targets the student who struggles with homework and effort during class instruction. The student may show a chronic inability to complete all homework, return books and assignments to school, and/or use good effort on assignments. Students benefiting from this type of plan may have initially performed well in class; they participated in some discussions and may have grasped some class assignments. However, they eventually begin to show signs of struggle as gaps in their knowledge jeopardize their ability to perform with their classmates and meet grade-level expectations. Preventing this type of snowballing problem is the objective of these types of plans. Unlike the other plans that cover the duration of an instructional unit or allow for a lengthier project-based assignment, these plans can be used for any length of time. Two to three weeks worth of these types of plans could be stapled inside a student's homework journal or notebook and be replenished as needed.

(Text continues on page 105.)

Figure 4.4. Broad Student-Guided Plan (Version 1)

Sarah's Daily Progress
(* 2 points each)

Morning

_1_ Assignment notebook signed by parent/homework completed/ materials in school

_2_ Completed all class assignments appropriately

_2_ Attentive and on task

_2_ Showed best effort on all work and made up any missed work (music lesson, etc.)

_2_ Participated well and worked well with others

_9_ /10

Afternoon

_1_ Completed all class assignments appropriately

_2_ Attentive and on-task

_2_ Showed best effort on all work and made up any missed work (music lesson etc.)

_2_ Participated well and worked well with others

_2_ Assignment notebook filled-in and materials prepared for home

_9_ /10

Total _18_

16–20 Very Good Day (full privileges)

11–15 Good Day (partial privileges)

10–0 Difficult Day (restricted privileges)

Comments:

Great job today, Sarah! Good participation in class discussion.

Figure 4.5. Broad Student-Guided Plan (Version 2)

At the end of every day, I will check to make sure I have all of my homework. I will bring home all folders I need together with my Take Home Folder.

___X___ Assignment notebook was signed by parent/homework completed/material in school

___X___ Completed all class assignments appropriately

	Monday	Tuesday	Wednesday	Thursday	Friday
Math	No	X	No	X	X
ELA	X	X	X	X	X
Science	X	X	No	X	X
Social Studies	X	X	X	X	X
Other	flute	library books	—	—	—

Comments:

Much better effort!

Kevin needs to bring math journal to class each day.

The Plan in Figure 4.4 (page 103) monitors assignments as well as behavior in the morning and afternoon. Often, students requiring this type of guidance are able to progress to a single late afternoon check once they have demonstrated ability to follow the plan. The Plan in Figure 4.5, uses subject areas as a way to monitor the student's homework assignments (or the student can self-monitor). Also included are prompts to remind the student of routine expectations. Both Plans include incentives—one allows privileges, whereas the other uses stickers. Although the plans are brief, they allow for much flexibility.

Simply noting infrequent problems that arise, as demonstrated by the teacher's note "needs to bring math journal to class" in Figure 4.5, is a perfectly acceptable way of addressing and resolving small matters without complicating a simple plan. Figure 4.4 (page 103) also makes use of the quick teacher note, "Great job today. Good participation in class discussion!" Teachers working with the Student-Guided Plans have numerous options for recording information on student progress, writing notes to address specific issues, and to provide encouragement.

A Peek into the Classroom

Nicole rarely completed her homework, especially if reading and/or writing activities were involved. Yet she had some solid test-taking skills and was able to just barely pass most of our unit tests in the first quarter of the school year. Because of this, my many notes and discussions with Nicole and her mother didn't raise much concern, especially as Nicole was still passing. Nicole's mother was also busy with a new baby and caring for younger family members and often forgot to sign Nicole's Assignment Notebook amidst her hectic schedule. Toward the end of the first quarter, Nicole often spent recess in study hall catching up, but even then, she didn't have enough time to make up all that she missed. By the second quarter it was clear that Nicole wasn't able to keep up with her peers. Her foundation wasn't strong enough. She couldn't build her content knowledge or necessary literacy skills when she lacked the basics which her classmates had developed through the review and practice exercises that my homework assignments provided. It was becoming clear that even her sufficient test-taking abilities could no longer get her passing scores on tests. I spoke to Nicole for some time, hoping to convey the effects of her lack of homework. She agreed that a plan in which she and I reviewed and checked her homework every morning was worth a try. Instead of having her mother sign her assignment notebook, I offered to sign it. I was surprised when she asked if I could give her a sticker every day she completed her homework using her best effort. She was a mature, independent student who I would have guessed had moved beyond the motivational lure of stickers. I was wrong. Following a quick check of her work, I gave her a sticker every morning that she had her homework in and completed using her best effort. Rocky at first, she met with more consistent success by the beginning of the fourth marking period. I suspected that the sticker was really of little value and that our quick chats together, no matter how brief and even routine, may have been the real lure.

Because of the careful and close monitoring afforded by the Plans in Figures 4.1 through 4.5, students who tend to benefit most from these have had persistent and recurrent difficulties. Reserving these types of Plans to no more than a few students is one way to safeguard their success and to keep them from becoming overwhelming in terms of time and attention. If too many are used, you may jeopardize their success; the reasons are as obvious as they are plentiful, and they all have to do with our most limited resource—time.

Solutions to Keep in Mind

- *Eliminate barriers*—Small issues may get in the way of succeeding with a Plan. If possible, eliminate the problem and consider other options to replace it. For example, if a student is not successfully meeting *all* components of a plan, make adjustments and move on. If parents or caregivers are unable to carry through with tasks within their student's Plan, seek their permission to involve others. Having a student's assignment notebook signed by an after-school daycare provider may need to be an acceptable alternative. Creating an incentive system that can be carried out at school can also be possible. For example, shooting hoops with the principal can be a great reward for some students.

- *Location…location…location…!*—Consider where students should keep their Plans. Make them easily accessible and try to build in routine. Although we've found that the Plans usually help most students, the rare exception is if the student does not assume responsibility for his or her part in the process. Specifically, students who are unable to bring their Plan to a teacher for signing, discussing behaviors, assigning points earned, or to review materials, the Plan's effectiveness is jeopardized. (Of course, some allowance needs to be made to help students transition into the process.) Building routine into the new process may be challenging at first, but eventually it should take hold.

- *Record keeping*—The Plans can serve as a helpful reference for students and teachers and should be kept and filed; they quickly remind us of successes as well as strategies that may have been unsuccessful, and they can establish cause-and-effect relationships between behaviors and outcomes. Keeping a student's completed Plans in a file folder ensures that you'll have them to help reinforce and encourage continued positive improvement.

- *Plans must be viewed as doable and fair*—Students will be quick to let you know if something is impossible or unfair. Ensuring that the academic and behavioral expectations outlined in the Plans are feasible will be a matter scrutinized by students. Another is that the incentives must match the expectations. Figure 4.6 has suggestions for family-based incentives and methods of distributing them which can be built into a Plan. Figure 4.7 (page 108) identifies some school-based incentives. In our experience, we've found that students must believe that they can accomplish what they are setting out to do, and they must also believe that it will be worthwhile. Both notions also strongly support the need to involve the student in creating Plans; encouraging their involvement also encourages their ownership.

Figure 4.6. Ideas for Incentives and Systems for Distribution

Incentive Ideas (Rewards, Recognition, and Privileges)

Hobbies

♦ *Collections* (build an existing collection)—baseball cards, Legos, polished rocks, stamps, stickers, coins, toys, dolls, action figures, cars, models, special animals, etc.

♦ *Athletic Interests* (planning a special sporting activity, enrolling in local classes, signing up for a local team sport, attending spectator events, or arranging a friendly play-off event at home and inviting friends)—soccer, baseball, ice-skating, horseback riding, swimming, karate, etc.

♦ *Crafts* (sign-up for a class, participate together in an activity, host a craft activity and invite a few friends, get new supplies).

Spending Time Together—with Family and/or Friends

♦ Game Night—select games to play with family and/or friends.

♦ Movie Night—rent a new movie, watch a family favorite, or borrow one you always wanted to see from the library.

♦ Special Dinner—plan a favorite meal at home or go out to a special restaurant

♦ Ice Cream Sundaes—concoct a new favorite

♦ Reading Together—from comic books to family favorites

♦ Campfire Night & Toasting Marshmallows

Extra Special Time for Favorite Activities

♦ Additional time to play video games, watch TV, talk to friends, use the computer, etc.

Special Adventures

♦ Outdoor Activities—camping, hiking, boating, water activities

♦ Trip to amusement parks, museums, special sites, etc.

♦ Sleepovers with a friend

♦ Painting pottery, making jewelry, crafts, and other special activities

Special Treats/Wishes

♦ Rewards can be toys, activities, games, or events that have special value for a variety of reasons.

(Figure continues on next page.)

Systems for Distribution

Point Systems

- All activities are given the same amount of points and a minimum number must be achieved over a period of time.

- Activities are given different points based on a perceived value (for example, demonstrating appropriate behaviors in math might be perceived as more important than doing so during recess) and a minimum number must be achieved over a period of time.

- Targeted activities are given different points based on difficulty level (for example, if recess is challenging due to the peer activities it might receive more points)

Graduated Point Systems

- Points (and incentives) might be presented using a tiered scale. For example, accumulated points could fall within one of multiple ranges, each range having its own corresponding incentives. Higher ranges would have incentives that are perceived to be of higher value.

Check & Tally Systems

- If a point system becomes discouraging, a check or tally system that is mildly more forgiving might be a place to start. For example, if a student has difficulty following instructions for an entire activity period, but is nonetheless making some progress, using a check system for "most of the time" (with the goal to get a check in a majority of the behavioral prompt areas) might be a more realistic way to recognize small improvements until a point system can be used.

Figure 4.7. Ideas for School-Based Incentives

Recognition Systems—Rather than rely on material rewards, incentives can certainly be based on recognition. Some planning might need to be worked out with the school and some consideration might be given to establishing recognition systems at school where a student can be recognized by his or her teachers, peers, and family.

Students can be recognized by:

- Receiving an invitation to lunch with a parent, teacher, or administrator.

- Participating in a special activity with a teacher, such as helping with a task or being "the assistant" for a specific lesson.

- Participating in a special activity with another school professional, such as shooting baskets with the principal, helping deliver mail in the office, etc.

- Participating in high-profile activities, such as reading the morning announcements over the loudspeaker, being a helper to other school professionals, leading a special schoolwide event, etc.

- Reading to a younger class or helping a younger class with an activity.

- Receiving praise from teachers or former teachers.

- *Start slow and proceed with caution*—Keeping in mind that the behaviors of this group of students may be the most difficult to change, it's important to set realistic expectations. In our experience, trying to change every challenging behavior at once is unrealistic. You might wish to prioritize behaviors and use an incentive system to align with this. Figure 4.8 contains examples of outcomes and expectations that might be helpful. Determine which behaviors you believe will bring about the most significant change, or select one in which the student will be successful, or use other appropriate criteria. While working on improvement in one area, be prepared for lulls in other areas.

Figure 4.8. Literacy Outcomes and Expectations

Writing

- I review my work to check neatness and readability.

- I check all of my work for spelling and use spelling resources when needed.

- I reread my writing to check grammar and accuracy.

- My writing is well organized and in the correct sequence.

- I use proper paragraphs.

- I include an introduction and a conclusion.

- I maintain a clear focus.

- My main idea is obvious.

- I use sufficient supporting details.

- I make meaningful connections.

- My writing shows style and voice.

- I use interesting vocabulary.

Reading

- I monitor my reading and use my strategies when I am confused.

- I think about the genre I'm reading and use helpful strategies I've learned.

- I keep in mind the purpose for my reading.

Listening

- ♦ I monitor my listening and do my best to avoid distractions.
- ♦ I listen carefully and collect important information.
- ♦ I take careful notes.

Keep in mind that expectations should be appropriate to the students' unique needs and that often social and emotional needs must be met before academic needs.

- ♦ *Keep the plans flexible and change can happen (providing your changes won't be perceived as unfair or impossible by the student)*—Situations may arise that cause you to have to change a Student-Guided Plan. The family situation might change, affecting how you work with family members—from the home-based incentives to who will be signing off on the Plan. New information might become available to you, causing you to rethink your strategies. Another possibility is that particular strategies might bring about unexpected changes that need readjustments; some you might wish to increase, while others may need to be diminished. Tailoring the Plan by making necessary changes only strengthens and supports its potential for success.

- ♦ *Beyond the beginning: Shortcuts to encourage autonomy*—Encouraging students to own and internalize the behaviors outlined in their Plans is the ultimate goal. Keep this in mind once you and your student(s) have made reliable progress. Consider ways to give them independence and to lessen your role. Streamlining a process, eliminating steps, having students give you a "thumbs up" in the morning if they've accomplished all expectations are ways students can assume more ownership. Cutting back on parent or caregiver signatures may be another way to transfer independence to the student. Keeping a mindful watch over this process is prudent; although we have met with success releasing some of our involvement in the review-and-guidance process with students, this is not universally true, and your attempts to do so may be premature.

Student Contracts

A Student Contract takes the Student-Guided Plan one step further and is a formal agreement you have with a student. It clearly states behavioral expectations or academic outcomes with goals that are intended to be long-term or permanent. Expectations and outcomes are also sometimes linked to incentives. For some students, the formality of writing down and signing an agreement might be a way to initiate change. Yet, there are many other positive collateral upshots that Contracts introduce, such as the following:

♦ They rely on having a sit-down, heart-to-heart talk with a student, which sends the message that their success matters. Knowing that a caring adult is mindful of their progress can help launch their improvement.

♦ Contracts represent one of the most tailored approaches to assisting a specific student with the student's specific needs. Every component in the Contract is unique.

♦ Contracts can help support other motivation-improvement strategies, such as those where parent involvement may be limited or unavailable, because the Contract is between you and your student. In our experience, involving parents, caregivers, or an influential relative usually strengthens the process of initiating positive change; however, we have not always been able to rely on parental involvement.

♦ Contracts can also come in handy when students are unable to or are disinterested in using a Student-Guided Plan (as discussed earlier, this lack of follow-through may jeopardize the Plan's success). For some students, using a Contract may be a step that precedes using a Student-Guided Plan. Although this may not be ideal, it may be an option that is worth trying.

♦ Contracts can also help initiate improvement in a targeted area—such as with a variety of literacy-based activities—especially when the student has long-standing and extreme pervasive motivational issues and you've decided that a workable starting point is needed.

♦ Like the Student-Guided Plans, Contracts are flexible and can also be reshaped to address an individual's needs, even when those needs change.

Figure 4.9 (page 112) illustrates a sample Contract that is used with a student who has struggled for many years with motivation difficulties. It is based on one originally created by Allen Mendler for increasing commitment (Mendler, 2000, p. 18). It also blends elements from Richard Sagor's "Goal Affirmation Sheet" (Sagor, 2003, p. 32). Here, however, the Contract is used to "increase effort," and it targets a student's performance within the student's literacy-based activities. Another significant change is that motivational incentives are linked to results. Other academic or behavioral expectations could be used in place of the guided reading activities shown in the first question in the figure: "Do you feel you are as successful as you could be with your guided reading activities?" For example, you might use a Contract to encourage a student to control behaviorial outbursts or to increase his or her attentiveness and participation. The suggestions that appear in Figure 4.8 (page 109) also can be used within a Contract.

Figure 4.9. Student Contract

Name _____ *Aaron Cloots* _____ Date _____ *November 5* _____

Contract for Increasing Effort
> *Aaron and I discussed that "effort" means the amount of time & the energy you put into something.*

> *Some ways to focus are:*
> *1. looking at the speaker*
> *2. ignoring distractions*
> *3. catching myself if I start to lose my place during reading*

1. Do you feel you are as successful as you could be with your guided-reading activities?

I'm not able to get all my work done and have to go to study hall to catch-up. I can follow along most of the time but when I haven't done the reading I have trouble following Ms. Bart. I guess I'm not as successful as I could be.

2. Are there areas you feel you could improve if you used more effort?

If I read more, it would help me get more information. If I had more information I could get ideas for questions that were asked. I could get my work done.

3. What is your plan for using more effort to improve these areas? (How will you do it? When will you do it?)

I'd like to get more information and use better effort. I can try to get what Ms. Bart means by staying focused during class and when I'm working at my seat. I could ask Lawrence to help me by reminding me to finish work.

> *Every other week, Aaron can draw near the computer stations instead of writing his Friday letter home.*

4. How can I or other people at school help you be successful with your plan?

I'd like a little more time to finish my work and maybe you could have me work somewhere that was quiet and had less distractions like the computer station. I might want to use a study divider if I can't ignore distractions.

5. What are some fair consequences that you should face if you choose not to follow your plan?

I might have to stay after school. Because of this, I won't be able to play with my friends. Although I wouldn't like that, I think it would be fair.

6. What are some rewards you would like to receive if you choose to follow your plan?

I would like some free time to draw. I really like to draw pictures about robots and heroes. I'd also like to use some colored pencils and stencils.

_____ *Aaron Cloots* _____   _____ *Ms. Bart* _____
(Student Signature)   (Teacher Signature)

Working Together to Complete the Contract

The teacher and student should complete the contract together. The probing questions launch insightful discussion between you and your student. Understanding your student is as critical. It is equally important that your student understand your concerns. Constructing a contract that is based on mutual understandings is the goal and, although this may seems like a simple and straightforward task, in our experience, some contracts end up being far from that. Although students may have "heard it all before" and claim to be all too familiar with teacher comments about their behaviors or performance, they may not fully understand the remarks or even have a clear picture of how their actions can jeopardize their ability to succeed. Should this be the case, they most probably don't understand their role in helping to initiate change. Straightforwardly discussing these matters may help to clarify a long-standing problem. Also, it's best to share these discussions at a time when you're not reacting to an immediate problem. This *distance* will be helpful. Finally, younger students often struggle to link causes and effects and truly grapple with understanding the connection between their actions and outcomes. Working to clarify this kind of disparity is often what takes place during your discussions.

Launching Your Contract

It may be necessary for you to clarify reasons why you would like your student to improve his or her effort in a certain area. Using the title of the contract as well as the first couple of questions will help you initiate discussions on effort and motivation. Discussions about answers to "Question 1: Do you feel you are as successful as you could be with your (targeted area of focus)?" and "Question 2: Are there areas you feel you could improve if you used more effort?" may take some time. As mentioned earlier, your student may have heard it all before, but the difference is that you now want them to discuss specific examples. Often, students will generalize and even parrot or mimic adult words or phrases, such as by saying their behavior is "inappropriate" or "unacceptable." Be prepared to calmly discuss some of the difficulties you've witnessed and observed. Students may agree with your assessment and acknowledge what you've witnessed or they may become defensive. Assuring them that your interest is in helping them may redirect the tone of the discussion. Still, be prepared to cite specifics, recent examples of situations that may have been regularly repeated. Figure 4.8 (page 109) presents suggestions for ways to describe in kid-friendly terms observable behaviors you have witnessed in your student.

Your Contract and How Others Can Help

Once you've been able to discuss responses to Questions 1 and 2, tackling ways to address the areas targeted for improvement is next. Here your efforts may need some support from others. First, it is important to align the problem with the proposed solution. Although this may seem straightforward, this step presents problems for most students and may be an area where you can provide helpful suggestions. Figure 4.8 (page 109) may provide some ideas, yet you may need to expand upon them. Considering ways to use resources available in your classroom and school will be helpful. Also, consulting with others within your district might also uncover other possible solutions.

Consequences and Rewards

Other interesting discussions generated by the contract are when students are asked to reflect on consequences (Question 5: "What are some fair consequences that you should face if you choose not to follow your plan?") and rewards they would like to receive (Question 6: "What are some rewards you would like to receive if you choose to follow your plan?"). This may be one of the first times that the student has deeply considered his or her role in affecting outcomes. Interestingly, some students are forthright in suggesting consequences that, although unpleasant, might initiate change. Others, when prompted to think beyond consequences that have already been tried and haven't worked, such as spending recess in study hall, a visit to the principal's office, or a temporary visit to another classroom, will suggest a unique and more personally motivating responses. Some examples are e-mailing a parent, losing school computer time, arranging weekly telephone calls, or meetings with a grandparent. (Additional discussions on negative consequences appear later in this chapter under "Tailored Consequences," page 123.) When students share this information, it demonstrates their willingness to bring about positive change and suggests that they don't enjoy their habitual struggles. They, too, welcome the hope change could bring.

Initiating discussions about rewards or incentives might also reveal information about a student that the teacher did not know before. Students may have interests, hobbies, or talents about which you may not have known. Working their reward idea into the contract is important and may take some creativity, especially as we would recommend that the reward selected be confined to the school grounds and be held during the school day. Some students may need help thinking of school-based rewards. Some of the ideas found in Figure 4.7 (page 108) may be workable. (Additional discussions on tailored motivational rewards appears later in this chapter under "Tailoring Your Incentive System," page 121.)

Documenting Your Ideas

Make notes right on the contract, even if you're still thinking about rewards or you're unsure of consequences and are considering one of several. You and your student need a new beginning, especially as other ideas you might have tried may not have worked well. Having detailed notes that reflect your thoughtful planning is one way to start. Also, making the best use of your time by continuously moving forward instead of rehashing the same matters (especially if you need to meet with your student several times to complete the contract) will be invaluable.

A Peek into the Classroom

Aaron rarely participated in class. He seldom spoke, and he hardly ever completed independent tasks. Instead, he would quietly daydream for long stretches of time or passively watch a classmate busily work—for as long as twenty minutes and sometimes longer—until I prompted him to join our class discussion or refocus his efforts on his own work. At times he claimed to be thinking about what someone had said or about his own work. Other times he shrugged his shoulders and said "sorry." Because of these problems he was unprepared for most classes and was falling dangerously behind. I wanted to try using a contract with Aaron and thought he would benefit most if we narrowed our focus to guided reading. He agreed that it might be helpful. As he read the questions and we began discussing the answers, I was surprised by many things: First, that he was unclear about the idea of "increasing effort," which I explained and noted on the contract, and, second, that he was able to identify why he wasn't as successful as he could be with guided reading—he couldn't follow his teacher's instruction because he didn't do the reading (which was assigned during class time)—yet he seemed completely unable to figure out a solution to the problem. I had to help him think through a plan that included ways to keep his attention on the teacher during instruction and other ways to minimize distractions caused by others so he could get his reading done (which included moving to a more isolated area and possibly using a study divider). We wrote everything down on his contract; he would write answers to the questions after we talked about them, and I would add ideas in the margins. I was also taken aback by his idea to stay after school with the principal if he didn't get his work done. At our school, staying after with the principal was rarely done. Still, it told me that he had little hope that his regular regimen of going to study hall during recess was going to change anything. Also, I was shocked to learn that he wanted free time to draw as a reward. I had absolutely no idea that he liked to draw. We worked out a plan that included this reward.

Follow-Up

How to follow-up with students who have contracts is as unique as the contract. Some students many need daily follow-up (like those who have Student-Guided Plans), whereas others may benefit from a brief teacher check that occurs less frequently. Initially, it might be best to meet briefly every day. You can provide positive encouragement and ensure that the student is following through with the contract.

One Final Thought: Turning Other Strategies into Contracts

Keep in mind that other strategies discussed in this book can be turned into contracts. For example, we have often used our tic-tac-toe boards within the Literacy Bins (discussed in Chapter 2) as a type of contract. In Figure 4.10 (page 116), specific activities we believe may be more beneficial to a particular student are highlighted or starred. This signals a student that he or she should complete the circled activities before selecting others. We also may ask the student to sign their tic-tac-toe board following a brief discussion of why those activities were selected for the student. The same is true for

Figure 4.10. Literacy Bin Contract

Name _Sarah Jackson's_   **Colonial Times**   **Tic-Tac-Toe**

Word Search Colonial Times	**It Happened When?** ☆Time Line Activity☆	**Genius TV Talk Show!**
Find and highlight all of the words from the word bank. Get ready to travel back in time!	Can you organize these important events into the correct chronological order? Use the dates as your guide. Look at the sequence of events that unfolds.	A scholarly showing of smarts (Library Pass Needed for Filming) Our extremely intelligent student scholars will share their "smarts" about common questions on the Colonial Period—live—on the popular talk show—"Genius TV." They've got smarts, they've got style…and just listen to them speak!
Colonial Leaders Hall of Fame!	**READ** _Read At Home!_	☆ **What Happened… And Why?** ☆ **Cause & Effect!**
Create a portrait of a leader to hang in the Colonial Hall of Fame and include a paragraph about your leader's accomplishments. Select from: Henry Hudson, Peter Minuit, Peter Stuyvesant, John Peter Zenger, Elias Neau, Samuel Fraunces, General George Washington, Joseph Brant, Saguyewatha, and George Clinton.	Have your parent sign your reading list of a minimum of five Colonial nonfiction books. _My Prairie Year_ and _Sarah Plain and Tall_ are works of historical fiction. You can swap either of these in place of _two_ nonfiction titles.	Use a cause & effect chart and find at least five examples in the book _New York as a Dutch Colony_ and then five other examples in the book _New York as an English Colony._
Drama!	☆ **DARE to Compare!** ☆	**Colonial Sites**
You will perform a one-person character play. Grab the spotlight and a book (Sarah Morton or Samuel Eaton) and tell your story (read it aloud) as if you were a Pilgrim child growing up in 1627. Practice, practice, practice, and perhaps you'll get a chance to record your play!	Compare & contrast Colonial school days to today's school days. Read "Colonial Schools" (an article) and _Colonial Teachers_ (a book) to help.	Visit some Colonial web sites where you can learn more about this fascinating time in our history. Record five new facts you've learned and let us know if you'd recommend this site to your classmates!

I Agree to Complete the Starred Activities Before Choosing Others

Sarah Jackson   Date _Feb. 19_

Student-Guided Plans. Although we've discussed the strengths of each device used as it is, we've also stressed each device's flexibility. Using any plan as a contract is acceptable. The formality of a personalized approach, a shared teacher–student discussion, and the actual act of signing a name to a document can have a meaningful and powerful affect on some students.

Solutions to Keep in Mind

- *I know I said I'd stay after school, but what I meant was...Transition time*—Hold students accountable for the plans they've agreed to in the contract. Nothing will discredit the value of your agreement more than altering it at the first sign of distress. Even though students need some time to transition into the arrangement, reinforce the student's role in helping to make the plan. You can also put a positive spin on the situation by letting your student know that sticking to the terms (and the contract as a whole) continues to demonstrate that there is a willingness on the student's part to bring about positive change—which is what it will ultimately take to succeed.

- *Avoid turning the classroom into a court of law*—We've found that addressing issues with a student who has a contract are best handled after some wait time. Confronting a student about the terms of your agreement as he or she is in the midst of an emotional outburst might not be the best time to enforce them. However, allowing some time to pass—anywhere from a minute to the end of a forty-five-minute period—might result in a better, more levelheaded discussion that will bring about positive results.

- *Your reaction matters more than you think*—Keep in mind that your reaction to an incident may either diffuse or ignite it. When working with students who have contracts, it's important they believe in your commitment to the contract through your actions and words. An emotional reaction may send the wrong message.

- *Changes may be warranted*—If, after you and your student have had some time to transition into the agreement—which could generally be anywhere from two to three weeks—you believe there is a need to alter components of the contract, such as consequences or rewards, don't hesitate to make changes. Be sure, however, that the changes are warranted and serve to promote the success of the contract. For example, a student may decide upon a different reward, or may like to add another strategy to the plan in Question 3. Both would serve to strengthen the contract. However, when a student suddenly decides that he no longer wants the consequence he helped devise, then that might not warrant change. Still, it should be discussed—once emotions have cooled and the immediacy of the problem has passed.

- *Make notes on significant points you discussed*—To avoid "did too" and "did not" disagreements, be sure to document all the main points you and your student discuss. Use the margins or add sticky notes if necessary. This will help subsequent discussions about your contract proceed smoothly.

♦ *Sharing your plan with others*—Although your contract is between you and your student, you may want to share a copy with others who are involved as part of either the reward or the consequence component. It might be helpful to initially discuss the ideas with them and wait through a transitional period before getting a copy of the contract to them. Their feedback is important and things could change.

Tailored Motivational Incentives

Even though this isn't a strategy that is often used in isolation, it is so vital to the success of all other strategies that it warrants separate discussion and action. Ironically, incentives play a pivotal role in the success of these motivational strategies, yet they may also be underexplored areas in terms of what we know about our students. What motivates our students? Many of us believe that our time is already stretched to its limits by our challenging and rigorous curriculums, the scope and volume of new information and technologies with which we need to become familiar, and our administrative duties. As a result, learning about a student's interest beyond the obvious is becoming a thing of the past. Some of us know little about our students' outside interests and hobbies, and what knowledge we do have is generally gained by reading over a pen-pal letter, a "how-to" descriptive writing piece, or another type of writing assignment that may have had specific parameters. Yet providing incentives that will entice a student relies greatly on our knowing this information and making use of it. In addition to that which we glean from our daily observations, this type of knowledge can be considered *essential information.* This section includes self-reflective exercises that you can use to assess your current knowledge about your students and determine to what degree you're using your knowledge in your daily instructional activities. Suggestions to help you strengthen and build both are also provided. Certainly, you may wish to give immediate consideration to your findings about those students who are most challenged by motivation issues. Designing an incentive plan for a particular student might be a pressing matter.

Figure 4.11 is a survey to help you determine how connected you are to your students. Can you respond to the questions with insightful information about all of your students, especially about those who struggle with motivation? Are there some questions where your knowledge is vague or lacking entirely? After reviewing the questions, you might wish to note where you seem to have gaps and determine a plan to get this information using the suggestions that follow.

Figure 4.11. How Connected Are You to Your Students? Survey

1. Do you know three to five mostly positive nonacademic facts about each of your students?

2. Do you know which of the core curriculum areas each of your students enjoys? Do you know which other curriculum activities interest your students (such as music, physical education, art)?

3. Do you know what types of school-sponsored or community-based activities and events your students participate in after school (sports leagues and instruction, community-based events, national organizations such as 4-H, Boy Scouts)?

4. Have you observed your students behavior

   ◆ during test-taking activities?

   ◆ while at play with others?

   ◆ during free time?

   ◆ while organizing materials?

   ◆ when seeking information?

   ◆ when solving problems?

   ◆ while working independently?

5. Are you aware of each student's social strengths as well as areas that might need support?

6. Have you made any rush-to-judgment decisions about any of your students based on data before meeting the student?

7. Have you ever questioned or disagreed with information presented in formal school records about any of your students?

8. Are you aware of what motivates each student?

9. Are all of your students ready and prepared to learn on a daily basis? Are there factors that may be interfering with any student's ability to participate and learn?

10. Are you aware of the best approach to take with your students to

    ◆ redirect their effort or attention?

    ◆ assist them with behavioral issues?

    ◆ support their ability to meet with academic success?

Ways to Learn About Your Students

There are numerous way to learn more about your students. Some are *informal* in that they may be infrequent, unplanned, and/or unintentional upshots of other curriculum activities. Others are *formal*, which are activities designed and used for the purpose to enable students to share information about themselves—with their classmates as well as with you, their teacher.

The following are examples of informal methods:

♦ *Casual observations*—Kid watching during class time, on the playground, in the cafeteria, in noncore classes, in home–school routines, on books they choose.

♦ *While reviewing/assisting with other work*—Reading response journals, etc.

♦ *Class discussions*—Connections they make and want to share.

♦ *The work or products produced in noncore classes*—For example, artwork and work from computer instruction.

♦ *Student letters, Friday letter home to parents and others*—Writing a Friday letter has become a routine in many of our fourth-grade classrooms. Here, students write to their parents or a caregiver about their week at school, providing feedback not only on what they did but what they liked (or didn't like) and more. Other letters, such as thank you letters used in, for example, a follow-up to a field trip, provide teachers an opportunity to glean other good insights into students' likes and dislikes as well as into their character—what matters to them, their values, and more.

♦ *Journal writing or free writing*—Many writing prompts can trigger a student's desire to write a personal response, which can provide you with great insights.

The following are examples of formal methods:

♦ *Chat journals*—Written correspondences shared between the student and you and/or others.

♦ *Electronic conversations*—Blogs and other electronic means of communicating ideas, thoughts, and opinions.

♦ *Surveys*—There's no harm in surveying students. Soliciting their feedback can be done after an instructional unit, at the conclusion of a major activity, or at any other time that seems appropriate. Because we often survey our students after an instructional unit, we've created a standard "Penny for Your Thoughts" form in which the students are asked to respond to their likes and dislikes.

♦ *Paired student interview*—A community-building activity often done at the beginning of the school year, students can interview one another about likes or dislikes, hobbies, etc., and then share this with others.

- *Interview parents and others*—Sending questionnaires home for parents or interviewing parents and caregivers is another way to learn information about your students. Although this type of information gathering is often done in early elementary grades, there's no reason that it can't be done at the middle grade level.

- *"All About Me" slideshow presentation, comic book, rap, monologues, self-portraits, and self-art*—These fun and artistic presentations can make available valuable information about your students.

- *Start-of-the-school-year games*—Tic-Tac-Toe Squares, Hopes and Fears, telephone, and other games. Many types of games and activities designed to introduce students at the onset of the new academic year are available and can be found in a variety of teacher resources, such as *Mailbox* and *Literary Spark*. Electronic websites to which your district might subscribe might be another good source for these kinds of activities.

- *Goals*—Having students set goals and write them down and periodically review their success attaining them throughout the school year is another good way to gain insights into your students.

- *Call for connections providing links to curriculum units of instruction*—This is a fun verbal activity in which a teacher can introduce a new area of instruction by simply mentioning the topic and then asking students to share any connections they might have with that topic.

- *Teacher–student journaling*—Methods to interchange written communication, such as a Classroom Mailbox, are other ways to learn information about your students.

Not only are there many other methods to use to gain information about students, but there are also many different variations on those listed above. Select methods that seem appropriate for your needs, are aligned with your instructional style, and may be easily integrated into activities you already have in place in your curriculum and/or classroom.

Tailoring Your Incentive System

Once you have methods in place and are collecting information about your students through formal and informal channels, you need to integrate their interests, likes and dislikes, and favorite activities into your classroom practices (see "A Final Note—Incorporating Your Findings into Your Classroom Instruction and Practices" below) and, more importantly, you also need to translate them into tailored incentives that can be used with any of the other motivational strategies presented in this book. This is especially true if you are seeking to design an incentive plan for a particular student. Referring back to Figures 4.6 (page 107) and 4.7 (page 108) will give you some ideas for incentives and rewards that might be a good match for a particular student. Offering novelty within an incentive system to those students who are most challenged by motivational issues is important, although sometimes simple actions and/or activities are best. Knowing your student well will determine what avenue you should take.

A Final Note—Incorporating Your Findings into Your Classroom Instruction and Practices

Figure 4.12 is another reflective survey whose questions are designed to help you consider how connected your instruction is to your students' interests and learning styles. Are your instructional approaches diversified? Are you reaching all students? Have you incorporated your students' interests to expand the curriculum beyond the classroom, giving it a real-world relevancy and application? Clearly these questions are probing and, after considering your responses, you might wish to note areas where you believe improvement could be made.

Figure 4.12. How Connected is Your Literacy Curriculum and Instruction? Survey

1. Do you use various technologies (blogs, web casts, tape recorders, radios, DVDs, video streaming, web scavenger hunts, etc.) for instruction?

2. Have you integrated award-winning books in your instruction?

3. Do you have a literacy-rich and welcoming environment in your room? (Does your collection of books reflect the diversity of your students' interests? Is the organization easy-to-grasp and are books in good physical condition?)

4. Do you have a method of introducing new literacy-based activities to the attention of your students, such as e-books, graphic novels, Reader's Theater, author streams, others?

5. Does your literacy program integrate content from other curricula areas in exciting ways?

6. When you model literacy-based activities (speaking, listening, reading, writing, viewing, and thinking) do you incorporate your students' activities or interests? Have you considered ways to make your lesson more motivationally appealing by making it applicable and connected to your students' interest?

7. Do your lessons reflect the interests of the various intelligences or modalities? Have you differentiated your instruction so that your materials, manner of delivery, and methods of instruction address the diversified learning styles of your students?

8. Do you allow opportunity for choice? Do your students feel successful and competent?

9. Do you conscientiously promote reading as an enjoyable activity?

10. Do you know timely and popular trends for the age level of the students you teach?

Solutions to Keep in Mind

♦ *Keep information handy*—You may wish to review information at a later time, especially if you've collected it during the early part of the school year as an early classroom community-building activity or getting-to-know-classmates activity. The need for you to assist specific students may not be readily known at that time.

♦ *Periodically update your findings*—We've found that intermediate-level students, like most students, change dramatically throughout the school year. What might have motivated them early in the year may no longer have the same appeal by the middle of the school year. Periodically keeping your information up-to-date by reintroducing any of the information-gathering methods discussed in this chapter will help keep information current.

♦ *How long and what happens next?*—The length of time your student(s) may need to be encouraged through incentives will vary. Your hope, of course, is that the success your student realizes will be cause enough for him or her to continue performing with improved effort, without the need for reward or recognition. If this is the case, you can certainly begin to remove the incentive component. Should there be a relapse in your student's level of effort, reinstate the plan. You might also wish to make some changes in the new plan to encourage new success. Taking cues from your students is the best way to determine how long you may need to keep the incentive system in place.

♦ *Changes may be necessary*—As discussed in earlier sections, students may wish to alter their reward or incentive. Don't hesitate to make these changes providing they serve to strengthen the Student-Guided Plan or Contract. Although you don't want to make perpetual changes that could slow down the success of the Student-Guided Plan or Contract, changes may need to be made. If circumstances make it impossible to carry out the incentive, change must be made. Being prepared to offer viable changes will help keep the Student-Guided Plans and Contracts moving forward.

Tailored Consequences

Begin With the Typical

Your classroom management system likely includes some type(s) of consequence, such as the following:

Notes home	Loss of recess	Visit to the principal's office
Loss of special activity	Study hall	Lunch in a separate location
Unable to attend events	Letters of apology	Parent involvement

Additionally, many systems also include an element of warning and then action. For example, missing homework three times may set into motion a consequence that previously was managed differently when it happened the first and second times. Even within this type of system, most teachers make allowances for special circumstances and alter or adapt their consequence accordingly.

Although these are just some types of consequence systems, there are many others. No doubt, you have your own classroom system, which may be linked to a schoolwide system, and the two work together to bring about varying degrees of success. These systems will be effective for some percentage of your classroom population. When they are ineffective, it's time to work through other consequences, especially for those students whose trouble may stem from motivational struggles.

Move to the Tailored

Just as you're able to tailor incentives to all students, especially to those challenged most by motivational struggles, so, too, can you tailor the consequences. The manner in which you choose to do this, however, may be quite different from the information-gathering actions you took to initiate your incentive program. Rather than determine negative consequences through formal and informal avenues described above, your initial efforts could be linked to the positive incentives you already have in place for these students. For example, if a student's incentive is to have free computer time, or to share his or her baseball card collection with the teacher one morning every week, then the consequence of losing that incentive (or privilege) may be consequence enough to encourage changed behavior. Beginning your consequence system by using plans linked to the incentive system still sends the positive message that your plan is effective and that reshaping behaviors may not require a more severe action. Here, too, it may be prudent to include a warning-and-then-action component, as well as a remediation component in the plan, the latter of which can simply be an exercise to encourage the student to reflect on the loss of incentive or privilege.

The next stage of consequence would be to discuss the situation honestly and openly with your student. As discussed in the *Student Contracts* section above, our experience is that students are fairly forthright—after what might amount to lengthy discussions in which facts and even documentation are presented in a nonconfrontational manner—in both acknowledging that the current system isn't working for them and also in suggesting alternative forms of consequence that might prove more effective. Working with their suggestions may be your best hope of bringing about positive change, as it not only places them in a position of contributing to their own success, but it also encourages their "buying into" the process. Some student-initiated examples of consequences include:

Change Physical Location	Staying After School
Contacting a Parent or Caregiver	Revising Assignments

The variety and scope of these suggestions supports the idea that matching an appropriate consequence to a particular student is important; an action that might cause one student to reconsider his or her actions will not necessarily have the same effect on another student. Despite the fact that students are contributing ideas, the solutions must still be respectful and appropriate, and the expectations must be reasonable. At times you might need to be the gatekeeper and prevent students from trying to include ideas that might stem from angry words or threats they might have heard from others inside or outside of school. Discussing why an idea may or may not be good to include in a Student-Guided Plan or Contract is worth having; it supports your words and actions that you intend these efforts to be successful, just as you ultimately intend the student to be successful with whatever changes you are attempting to bring about.

Novelty in Your Approach

As a final approach, the element of novelty might be worth trying. For example, if your school does not typically keep students after regular school hours, working out a special arrangement to have your student stay after school so he or she can complete tasks would be out of the ordinary. This consequence might be just enough to encourage some change in behavior. Another unique consequence might be to temporarily place the student in a different in-school setting, such as a colleague's classroom where the student can complete work in a separate, supervised location. However, it is still vitally important to remember that the novel and unique ideas must not challenge the parameters of being respectful and appropriate. Discussing these kinds of plans with your principal and then with the student's parents or caregivers ensures that everyone is onboard and in agreement with your objectives and ideas for initiating positive change.

Solutions to Keep in Mind

♦ *Mix and match your consequences*—We often use multiple consequences together to initiate change—some traditional with some tailored and even some novelty. As a result, it isn't necessary to impose harsh or unreasonable consequences simply because you've tried one after another and nothing seems to work. Clustering them together may prove a more suitable approach for bringing about change. For example, regularly scheduled parent visits with the principal (and the student) with intermittent notes home combines three ideas together. Determining why one strategy hasn't worked and then strengthening that weak area with another traditional strategy might initiate improvement.

♦ *Bring parents and caregivers onboard from the start*—Keeping parents or caregivers informed of your progress is necessary so they can support your efforts at home; however, it also may help should you need to try additional strategies, especially if those strategies require more of their involvement and participation. Having them onboard immediately may enable you to quickly and easily transition into a more aggressive plan of action.

♦ *What to do when you and your student don't agree on consequences*—If you and your student can't agree on consequences, try to arrive at a mutually acceptable plan that includes some give and take. For example, if a student is not providing suggestions yet is unwilling to accept any you provide, suggesting that a warning element be put in place might be more agreeable. For example, if a student does not want you to arrange for routine after-school sessions with the principal, include that something else will be tried once or twice before reverting to this. Doing so may save you having to manage confrontation and power struggles as you attempt to implement the consequence.

- ♦ *Avoid confrontations and power struggles*—Should problems arise when implementing the consequence of the Student-Guided Plan or Contract, try to minimize confrontation and power struggles with your student. Try redirecting a student's attention, offering some form of choice, interjecting humor, asking a question, providing positive reinforcement, reminding your student about previous successes, waiting quietly, and/or momentarily postponing your discussion but establishing a start time to resume.

- ♦ *Document your discussions and actions taken*—Although your consequences may be recorded on the Student-Guided Plan or Contract, you should document subsequent meetings and actions taken, especially when you're imposing consequences. This serves a number of practical purposes: Tracking your progress lets you know what works and what doesn't work and keeps your plan current and workable; you may need to refer back to concrete examples for subsequent discussions with students (especially if your plan includes a warning system and you are at the point of imposing a higher order consequence); and others may need to be kept informed and involved.

Mentorship

We considered ourselves fortunate that our superintendent valued the ideal of mentor programs for all new teachers who were hired in our district. He was touting the importance of mentoring long before such programs had been embraced as a viable, productive, and highly successful educational practice. Helping new teachers transition into the district and the classroom through a formal process enabled many of us to participate in some way, either as mentor—those providing the wisdom—or "mentee"—those who were on the receiving end of the wisdom. In addition, our district was located in an area in which there were several colleges and universities that offered teacher education programs. We often hosted college students who were working toward a degree in education. Perhaps because of both kinds of experiences, we were eager to try to establish some kind of mentor program that would serve the purpose of connecting a helper, an advisor, a caring adult with those students whose struggles with motivational and effort issues interfered with their academic success. Although this type of mentor program was different than the teacher-to-teacher programs with which we had experience, we hoped that those students who demonstrated highly unmotivated characteristics and behaviors might benefit from the influence and direction of a person whose primary reason for being there was to help them succeed. Overall, our results indicated the models that were so successful with teachers were also beneficial to students.

Different Mentorship Models

Working with mentors is an approach that can bring about positive change. There are many different types of mentorship models and their parameters are also very flexible. The models we find useful are diverse and are based on what we perceive as needs for our struggling students. For example, we sought the help of some mentors whose responsibility had been to support and encourage the student who is working through some type of positive change. In such cases, mentors do not know much of the history of the student's difficulties nor are they privy to all efforts undertaken by the teacher and others to help that student change. They assume a neutral position as listener and supporter, helping to rally almost from the sidelines for the student's success.

A Peek into the Classroom

Mrs. H. is an aide whose cheerfulness was exuberant. The students loved talking to her when they arrived at school. Her morning job was to assist with bus arrival and oversee the students as they entered the school building. She took a genuine interest in the students and asked about their weekend activities—how they made out at soccer or what games they taught their new baby sister, etc.—while she shuffled them into the building. I asked her if she wouldn't mind paying a little extra attention to Jared who left our district when he and his family relocated, but then returned three months later. He had trouble taking his work seriously and often disturbed others who sat next to him with his class-clown antics. Although Jared was smart, he had large gaps in background knowledge, which were causing him to fall increasingly behind. It seemed that his clowning around grew worse when he struggled academically. I had worked out a Student-Guided Plan with him that targeted improvement in his class behavior and in his homework responsibilities. I told Mrs. H. about these targeted areas and asked her if she wouldn't mind giving him some words of encouragement every morning when he arrived at school, which she did. Jared often remarked about his brief chats with Mrs. H. It was clear he enjoyed her involvement.

Other mentors have had more active roles which vary depending upon the student's unique circumstance. For example, a mentor might help a student with a particular task that, over time, has proven to be a challenge.

A Peek into the Classroom

Mr. Benavides was a graduate student who met with Steven every Tuesday from 2:30 until 3:00 for four months. Most of the time they worked on homework or classwork that needed to be finished. If they were able to get everything done, then sometimes they got to play games. Mr. Benavides reminded Steven that finishing his work would help him get good grades. It would also free up his time so he could do whatever he wanted at night, like talk to his friends, play outside, or other social things. According to Mr. Benavides, the best part of the mentoring program was being able to help younger students—academically and socially—and seeing them benefit.

Over a five-week period, Mr. Benavides saw Allison twice a week for about an hour. He usually helped her with math and English homework. He knew when he helped her she not only got better grades, but it helped build her self-confidence. He thought this made a difference.

Another model that is often used with students who struggle with more severe motivational difficulties is to involve the mentor in a Student-Guided Plan or Contract. In this model, the mentor may help design and/or administer any type of formal arrangement between the classroom teacher and the student. In essence the classroom teacher and mentor pair up to assist the student. Here, the mentor might help to provide positive encouragement; redirect a student who has difficulty taking corrective action according to the student's Plan; check on the student's progress with a particular task or behavior daily or as often as directed in the Plan or Contract; provide reassurance as needed; or assist in carrying out a consequence; among other tasks and responsibilities. Determining how to best help meet the needs of the student is the guideline to follow in establishing the mentor's responsibilities. The mentors who work with the students in this capacity might be the student's former teacher, a teaching professional, or some other education professional/administrator who has volunteered to be a mentor. Alternatively, the mentor could be a professional or paraprofessional at school who the student recommended and who agreed to participate in the mentorship program. You might wish to select a mentor who already works in the school, as he or she will have some familiarity with school policy, curriculum matters, and typical classroom practices, which will save you precious time explaining their importance.

A Peek into the Classroom

Ms. Felding, the school librarian, knew Jenny well and was familiar with some of her struggles with effort and motivation. She taught Jenny and her classmates last year during their weekly library special, and she often supervised Jenny whenever she went to the library to complete her work or finish her tests. She was upbeat and positive as she encouraged Jenny to stay focused and attentive so she could complete her work. Jenny required a lot of prompting. She was not surprised when Jenny's teacher asked if she might consider being Jenny's mentor, and she agreed. Ms. Felding worked with Jenny and Jenny's teacher to create a Student Contract that documented Jenny's goals to improve her focus and attentiveness, rely more on using her prewriting organizational tools (as lengthier written tasks seemed to be her greatest challenge), and to monitor her time. Ms. Felding was familiar with the district's graphic organizer that was used for writing and was able to help Jenny for twenty minutes each morning, three times a week, which coincided with Jenny's daily language arts writing block. Ms. Felding and Jenny also planned to note the amount of time it took Jenny to complete sections of the graphic organizer, hoping to see improvement as Jenny gained skill with the task. This also enabled Jenny's teacher to quickly and easily monitor

Jenny's progress simply by reviewing the completed organizer. The three also devised a list of tips Jenny could use whenever she became distracted:

♦ Remove "distractables" from work space (erasers, pencil sharpeners, jewelry, hair bands, etc).

♦ Focus my attention on the task (use my finger to "hold my place" on the task).

♦ "Talk-out" the task to guide my thinking.

Ms. Felding copied this list on the margin of Jenny's graphic organizer as a reminder. Ms. Felding, Jenny, and Jenny's teacher decided to meet for a five-minute discussion during recess on Mondays and Fridays to touch base. Meanwhile, Jenny's teacher reinforced these same ideas (and others) during Jenny's regular classroom instruction.

Solutions to Keep in Mind

♦ *Consider suitable matches*—You improve the chances of having a successful mentor program if the mentor and student are able to connect in a positive way. If you don't already know the mentors (some may be working through a high school program, a community volunteer program, are retired teachers, or are involved in a Foster Grandparent Program), spend some time informally talking to them so you can make a good partnership matches.

♦ *Don't hesitate to make changes in your mentorship program*—After you've started the mentor program, if you determine that the mentor partnership isn't working, don't hesitate to make adjustments: rework the responsibilities, alter the frequency of meetings, or consider a replacement mentor. Remember that the objective of the mentorship program is to help the student, and if that isn't happening, change is needed.

♦ *Be aware of school policy*—Make an appointment with appropriate administrators to discuss any policy that could affect your mentorship program. For example, students may need to be directly supervised by a certified teacher at all times, which could mean that your high school mentor might need to work with students while you're present in the classroom. Also, it is important to be aware of requirements such as having parents sign a letter or agreement allowing their student to be involved in the program.

♦ *Continuing your mentor relationships into subsequent years*—If you've been able to establish a successful mentor relationship, you may want to pass along this information (together with any Student-Guided Plans and Contracts) to the teacher who will be working with the student in the following year. It may be a good starting point for next year, although the teacher may want to reserve judgment until he or she feels confident that evidence supports its continued use—things can change significantly (a point discussed in the first vignette in this chapter).

Common Ideas Among the Strategies for Helping the Highly Unmotivated

As is evident, many of the strategies and/or tools that are used to help those students who are significantly challenged by motivational issues are individualized and tailored to a particular student's needs. Still, there are many commonalities among them, all of which greatly contribute to their success.

- *They are flexible*—As stated in many areas throughout this chapter, the tools are very flexible and can be shaped to meet the needs of many students. This flexibility addresses the reality that students' needs may be very different. Having tools that can be individualized and tailored to a student may be our best hope for affecting change.

- *They recognize varying levels of progress and consequence*—Nearly all actions that result from the use of these tools are recognized. It is important to reward even small improvement. It is equally important to have a system of consequences where all is not lost, but instead there is some reason to remain engaged in trying.

- *Many strategies rely on frequent monitoring that could extend over a lengthy period of time*—Although our hope is that each student will eventually use the strategies and skills we've practiced together to become autonomous and independent learners, this process can be a lengthy one. We typically see improved performance from most students, although their progress is not without many ups and downs along the way, especially at the start. It's difficult to distinguish if this group of students requires our continued and extended support or if other benefits such as the opportunity to work closely with a caring adult(s) at school, is something they want to hold onto.

- *Many include involvement of others*—Success is often realized through the help and support of many people.

- *The tools and strategies affect the whole child*—These tools often reach into social, behavioral, and academic areas of the child. The need to bring an almost harmony among all of these areas is clearly evident.

Motivation Improvement Initiative Tip #7: Determine Which Student(s) Might Benefit Most from One of These Strategies and Devise a Plan of Action to Assist the Student(s)

In determining how to incorporate these strategies into your Motivation Improvement Action Plan, you might want to begin by determining which students you feel might benefit most from these highly individualized strategies. You might already have tried some strategies of your own or even some that are presented in earlier chapters in this book and found that they were not as effective as you hoped. You might also recognize in several of your students the same or similar characteristics of students in the classroom vignettes or in the description at the beginning of this chapter. Determining which students you think will benefit may take some careful consideration.

Although it's difficult if not impossible to predict the number of students whose needs will best be met through one or more of the strategies presented here, our experience is that this number may be less than twenty-five percent of the class. In our average class size of twenty students, roughly two to three students may be supported through these methods. Meanwhile, the other strategies described in Chapters 2 and 3, are to varying degrees effective for motivating seventy-five to ninety percent of the class.

You might want to begin by selecting one or two students and design a tailored plan using any of the information-gathering tools discussed in this chapter. On your Motivation Improvement Action Plan you are only tentatively planning and noting your ideas, as many of the details will be worked out between you, your student, and possibly other collaborators. Still, it might be helpful to record your tentative ideas about your student's behaviors, the strategies you think might be most effective for that student, and your knowledge of that student's interests. This exercise will also enable you to determine what information may need to be gathered.

Figure 4.13 features the Motivation Improvement Action Plan in which tentative plans were created for two students, Vincent and Amanda, incorporating Tip #7.

Figure 4.13. Motivation Improvement Action Plan Sample with Tip #7

Underdog Strategies	
My Successful Strategies	Those Strategies I'd Like to Try
1. *Additional computer time*	1. *Goal setting display board*
2. *Homework pass*	2. *New technology use – digital camera*
3. *Special treats*	3. *Group snack*
4. *First in lunch line*	4. *Friday games*
5. *Reading chair privileges*	5. *"Do-overs"*

Strategies for the Highly Unmotivated—General Planning for One to Two Students

Vincent

Targeted Behaviors: *Outbursts*
Organization

Strategies: *Student Plan*
School-Based Recognition

Interests: *comic books*
electronic games
action figures

Amanda

Targeted Behaviors: *Homework*
Effort

Strategies: *Student Contract*
Involve Parents

Interests: *art*
animals
sticker collection

Notes: *Vincent makes good progress when he receives individualized support and is reminded of appropriate behaviors.*

Amanda is motivated by animal stickers.

How Would You Motivate These Students?

Case Study #4: Devon

Devon was often absent from school. Other times he arrived late, long after we started a lesson. Then, he settled in by unpacking his materials and looking for a pencil. By the time he was ready to join us, the lesson was nearly over. When he finally settled in, he was very quiet and rarely volunteered to read, even after a classmate helped direct him to the correct page. He also rarely raised his hand to answer questions. He was very quiet and never drew attention to himself. Devon was falling behind in all of his reading and writing assignments and he didn't seem to care. When he was able to complete a writing task, his work was often brief and showed little effort. He had a history of this behavior. (See Appendix A, page 144, for an outcome of Case Study #6: Devon.)

Case Study #5: Renee

Renee let out a huge, exaggerated sigh and rolled her eyes as if to punctuate that she did not intend to do what I asked. If I persisted, she outwardly defied me, even when I offered her choices, a strategy she quickly foiled by refusing to select any. She was argumentative and often tried to invite confrontation not only with me but with classmates as well. She brought many outside problems into class and didn't seem ready or able to leave them at the door. Already she seemed defeated, and she hadn't even reached the sixth grade. (See Appendix A, page 144, for an outcome of Case Study #7: Renee.)

Case Study #6: Sam

Sam was the youngest student in class, and his behavior often reflected this. He continuously needed reminding to walk correctly—not skip, jump, prance, or hop—as our class moved through the hallway. Most fourth-graders could master this quickly. Yet everyday, Sam and I were in a well-matched game of tug of war; my reminders would pull him away from his imaginary world of horseplay, but as soon as my back was turned, he retreated to his action-packed world. This was the way it was for everything; while everyone else in the class was working silently on their independent-reading activities or a writing assignment, he suddenly chattered to himself in baby talk. Like his carefree prancing through the hallways, he was unable to control this. He just wasn't at the same level of readiness as the others. (See Appendix A, page 145, for an outcome of Case Study #8: Sam.)

5

Frequently Asked Questions

This chapter contains answers to some of the questions we are most frequently asked in our workshops. Also included are some of the more difficult questions we struggled with while shaping the strategies described in this book to address the unique needs of our students. At the end of our workshops we always allow time for questions and answers and typically find that participants are at varying stages of building their collection of useful strategies for increasing student effort and motivation. We hope that the answers to these questions will help you keep moving forward.

♦ *Question:* How can I fit motivation related activities into my already busy schedule?

Answer: Many motivational activities can be built into your routine or daily plans. Offering choices, completing charts, working in groups, and varying modalities can all be a typical part of your day. Including them in your routines or daily plans strengthens their effectiveness as they become a part of existing classroom processes and your instructional procedures. Extra activities can be scheduled monthly or quarterly and can be held during lunch, recess, or other noninstructional time.

♦ *Question:* How can I best utilize support staff to improve motivation?

Answer: Many motivational activities can be adopted schoolwide or across many classes or grade levels. Different teachers can be given responsibility for maintaining special bulletin boards, hosting literacy-based celebrations, performing other tasks routinely; special area teachers (e.g., those who provide instruction in library, art, physical education, or music) can encourage student participation in the activities, include some or other similarly appropriate activities in their classrooms, and also participate in most activities. Many students look forward to recognition and/or participation from the principal, special area teachers, community members, and parents.

♦ *Question:* What is the difference between "unmotivated" and "highly unmotivated" students?

Answer: Students who demonstrate highly unmotivated behaviors may not respond to some of the typical motivators that are appropriate for their grade level (e.g., praise, good grades, and rewards). Also, their lack of motivation is often pervasive, affecting all or most academic areas as well as social areas. Many have also have struggled with motivation difficulties for some period of time.

♦ *Question:* Why does it seem that lack of motivation is becoming a bigger problem with each passing year?

Answer: There is a wide range of reasons why motivation seems to be hindering more students' achievement each year. Standards and expectations continue to change requiring students to raise their performance. Outside stimulation and activities, such as television and video games, may make it more difficult for students to focus, or may cause them to spend less time on academics. Additionally, students have busy after-school schedules, which are increasingly demanding of their free time. It also seems that there are more distractions during the school day that may interfere with classroom routines. In sum, we may not be able to pinpoint exactly what is causing the decline in motivation, yet we must attempt to address the challenge.

♦ *Question:* Isn't it unreasonable to expect that high-need students will show the same motivation as students who reach academic success with ease?

Answer: No. We find that our struggling students often show the best overall effort. We often encourage students to set personal goals and to make forward progress. It is important to help each student recognize his or her effort separate from his or her grades.

♦ *Question:* What can I do during a lesson to improve student motivation?

Answer: Offering students many opportunities to stay active and participate in class rather than sitting passively increases the likelihood that they will stay engaged. Allowing for student-selected activities and assessments also improves students' connection with the class and raises motivation. Pacing lessons in a way that allows students success and repeated practice helps to build confidence, which also helps with motivation.

♦ *Question:* What if my school doesn't supply funds for rewards/prizes?

Answer: Praise, displaying work, photos, names on a bulletin board, sending a note home, earning free time, and special events are all motivational rewards that have no cost. Other methods of funding incentives could be through your Parent-Teacher Association or by using your teacher book club incentives, such as using your accumulated points to buy books or other incentive offers, including *freebies* (free products or materials) that are available to teachers.

♦ *Question:* When can I expect to see results? For how long might I need to support a student?

Answer: These are difficult to determine as the answer to both questions is based on the uniqueness of each student's needs. Although you might see positive results immediately, we often see inconsistent growth at the onset of working with a student as the student learns new skills and perhaps struggles to make changes to long-standing behaviors. The length of time you may need to support a student can be determined as you begin to try to gradually lessen it. Should you need to try again, simply adjust your routines as necessary (possibly with some minor changes) and go forward. Remaining flexible is critical. Additionally, some practices may be intermittent, whereas others become part of your routine.

♦ *Question:* Can these activities be used in subsequent grades as students move from grade level to grade level?

Answer: Yes. Teachers at higher grades levels can review how the activities, strategies, and tools were used at the lower grade level and plan to either include them at the higher level and/or adapt them in a way that might be more age appropriate. They can also link them to the students' higher-level curriculum.

♦ *Question:* Will these activities, strategies, and tools be effective if I'm unable to get assistance from my colleagues or from a student's parents or caregiver?

Answer: Yes. You can easily integrate many of these activities and plans into your classroom routines without the assistance of others, yet some are better designed for districtwide use and/or some degree of involvement from colleagues. We recommend always seeking family or caregiver support. Even if they are unable to participate in an ideal way, their support is valuable and necessary. It is also important to note that many of the strategies encourage students to gradually assume responsibility for their success.

♦ *Question:* If we provide too much support might we be encouraging a student's learned helplessness?

Answer: No. Although this may be a concern, the *Gradual Release of Responsibility Model* (Pearson & Gallagher, 1983), which has proven effective for different kinds of academic instruction, seems a valid model to apply to the more tailored strategies—Student-Guided Plans and Contracts—which involve instruction (for example, learning new behaviors to replace existing behaviors). However, if this model is not used, the possibility may exist. Keeping in mind that your initial effort and subsequent support may be very different for each student—what works for one student, may not work for others—is a way to keep in check your need to monitor each student carefully as you begin to lessen your support.

♦ *Question:* Might our best intentions to encourage student motivation backfire if others disagree with the process?

Answer: Although this is a possibility, keeping other professionals and parents involved and abreast of the motives and goals should lessen the chances, even if others are unable or unwilling to assist your efforts. Carefully documenting and monitoring the plan and making adjustments when needed is essential.

♦ *Question:* How might you coordinate the use of all of these activities, strategies, and tools among all students in a classroom?

Answer: The Superhero Strategies and Underdog Strategies are integrated into our classroom routines and help to motivate and encourage improved effort in the majority of the students. The strategies used with students demonstrating highly unmotivated behaviors—the Student-Guided Plans and Contracts—are used with relatively few students. These figures vary from year to year and from class to class.

♦ *Question:* Are you always successful in helping every student with these activities, strategies, and tools?

Answer: No. Although we see varying degrees of improvement in nearly all students with whom we've worked, there are some students whose lack of progress warrants further action. In such cases, working together with school and outside professionals may be necessary. They can initiate contact with other outside support resources who are qualified to assist in ways beyond the scope of this book. Keeping your principal involved in all of your plans is one way of knowing when the involvement of school professionals as well as outside professionals may be appropriate.

♦ *Question:* What role do state standards play in your strategies and in your instructional approaches discussed in the book?

Answer: Our state and district are very standards based, and we are required to document the standards that align with the content of our instruction, as well as support our selection of instructional methods. In addition to this, teachers and administrators within our district have completed the lengthy process of creating curriculum maps for grades K through 12. These maps not only demonstrate our alignment to state standards, but also reflect our accountability for accurate grade-level progression of curriculum content. All discussions regarding instructional content and methodologies are supported within this context.

Appendix

Case Study Outcomes: How We Motivated These Students

Featured below are the outcomes to case studies that have appeared throughout the book. Page numbers have been provided indicating where each case study appears. The studies were introduced within specific chapters as they captured student behaviors, attitudes, or actions discussed in that chapter. By introducing the case studies like this, we share our experience and also let you know that you're not alone in your struggles with motivation-based literacy issues.

The students in the case studies probably seem familiar to you; they reflect actual situations we've encountered over time—either directly or through shared experiences with other professional who have grappled with motivational issues. They represent "typical" problems many of us have encountered. The case studies may help you develop a sense that your mission to troubleshoot similar motivation-related literacy problems and affect change is one shared by many professionals in education. Just knowing this somehow makes the task less daunting.

Just as we introduced the case studies in specific chapters for specific reasons, we also intentionally placed the outcomes in the back of the book. This enabled us to discuss techniques that may not have been introduced until much later. We hope this system is helpful, and we invite you to refer back to the studies whenever they may prove useful.

Outcome of Case Study #1: Mina (page 25)

It was clear that Mina had poor work habits and was capable of achieving much more than she did. Additionally, she had some very strong skills, such as her "take-charge" attitude, her assertiveness, and her ability to pickup information easily, all of which may have concealed and possibly even contributed to her weak study and work habits. Now her methods of operating were no longer working, and she was ill-prepared to change—the skills she suddenly needed to be successful were not available. To help Mina, we discussed the need for her to develop these other skills, and we asked her parents to assist at home by working with her to establish an after-school routine to get her homework done while also completing all other responsibilities (we learned Mina was responsible for assisting with a younger sister). We also held her more accountable for completing homework assignments and asked to see her assignment notebook daily. If her parents were unable to sign it, we agreed that a teacher could sign it providing the work was acceptable. Additionally, Mina received targeted praise for assignments in which she clearly demonstrated improved use of these skills. Mina's performance was monitored throughout the school year.

Outcome of Case Study #2: Kirk (page 25)

Kirk had both behavioral and social difficulties, as well as academic troubles, and often they were inseparable. With his parents' permission, we included Kirk in one of the school-based groups that helped students to develop appropriate social skills. He met twice monthly with this group during his lunch and was provided with strategies to help him respond to classmates, teachers, and other adults appropriately. We also created a daily Student-Guided Plan for Kirk that, based on a point system, served to reward Kirk if he met behavioral and academic benchmarks. Kirk moved from class to class with his checklist, which he kept stapled to the inside of his assignment notebook. All of his teachers were involved in helping to monitor Kirk's progress and took part in completing his checklist. We also assigned a student volunteer to help Kirk organize his desk on a routine basis.

Outcome of Case Study #3: Jennifer (page 25)

We worked with Jennifer's mother and arranged for Jennifer to receive breakfast at school. Rather than eat in the cafeteria, Jennifer was asked to eat in the classroom (along with other students) so she wouldn't miss any of the morning work and also so the teacher could quickly check to see that her homework was complete. Although the teacher touched base with Jennifer daily to check that she completed her assignments, she only looked at specific assignments on a periodic basis. When Jennifer did not complete her work, she was asked to complete it in study hall, where she was monitored by the study hall teacher. Jennifer was assisted in this manner throughout the school year.

Outcome of Case Study #4: Devon (page 133)

Devon's overall interest in school was low. We needed to take advantage of every opportunity to show him that he was capable of doing well. We asked Devon to help us create a daily Student-Guided Plan outlining what he needed to do. This included, among other things, completing more assignments, improving his class participation, improving his effort on his lengthier written assignments, and a conscious effort to settle in quickly. We also assisted him in creating a schedule to help him manage his time. Scheduling in recess and music lessons enabled him to see that his day wasn't too overwhelming and that there were several things he really enjoyed. Each day Devon monitored his progress and evaluated himself in his Plan. At first, he had much more incomplete than complete work, and he sometimes admitted his effort wasn't up to his ability. However, we praised his accomplishments and offered suggestions to help him improve. We could see his pride when he filled in more on his Plan or was praised for quality work or participation. It seemed to be a matter of changing old habits. Although the process was slow, it was steady. We continued to monitor Devon throughout the following school year and were pleased to see that he continued to apply most of his new strategies.

Outcome of Case Study #5: Renee (page 133)

Renee had learned many bad habits and also lacked positive role models. A combination of responsible peer role models, informal peer mentors, and a daily Student-Guided Plan contributed to her future success. Renee was offered many opportunities to eat lunch in the classroom with her classmates and teacher. During this time positive attitude and academic goals were discussed. Renee listened as her classmates told of their struggles and how they solved their problems. Renee was able to see that she wasn't alone in her difficulties. She began to develop a newfound respect for her work, as well as new peer relationships from which she could seek support when needed. Although

Renee got little support from home, we worked hard to keep her mother involved by asking her to sign Renee's assignment notebook and her daily Student-Guided Plan. Renee's attitude toward school was quickly turned around, and she effectively used her Plan to monitor her own progress. It was hard to believe the difference in Renee after only a few weeks.

Outcome of Case Study #6: Sam (page 133)

Sam's academic struggles were documented back to his earliest days in school. His records show him struggling through his primary years, both academically and socially. He received extra support services from school and had attended our district's summer enrichment program every year. We tried several of our motivation strategies to help improve Sam's issues. We paired him with a few caring adults in our building who asked him about his work, offered him assistance with organization and homework, and offered him extra attention and support. Although this process didn't address all of our concerns, it did seem to help keep Sam slightly more focused than he had been. We also set up regular meetings with Sam's mother. She shared our concerns and let us know that some family difficulties often contributed to Sam's academic issues. She also shared our concern about his immature behavior and explained that because of his late birthday he started school at age four, and that she had always wished she had started him in school a year later.

It was agreed that Sam's tasks would be broken down into short intervals, which we would help him monitor through a Student-Guided Plan, and he would be allowed opportunities to move around the class unobtrusively as an incentive. Sam was given the choice of where to sit to avoid distractions, and we helped build into his Plan a chart to organize his materials and assignments. Although Sam's difficulties did not disappear, he made steady progress.

Appendix

Motivation Tools

Motivation Improvement Action Plan

Starting Point: _____

_____

Goals:

- _____
- _____
- _____

Collaborators: _____

_____

Philosophy Statement: _____

_____

_____

_____

Expression of the Ideal: _____

_____

Superhero Strategies:

1. _____

Ways to Adapt: _____

_____

_____

_____

Collaborators: _____

_____

2. _____

Ways to Adapt: _____

_____

_____

_____

Collaborators: _____

_____

Motivation Improvement Action Plan

Underdog Strategies	
My Successful Strategies	Those Strategies I'd Like to Try
1.	1.
2.	2.
3.	3.
4.	4.
5.	5.

Strategies for the Highly Unmotivated—General Planning for One to Two Students

Targeted Behaviors: _____   Targeted Behaviors: _____

_____   _____

_____   _____

Strategies: _____   Strategies: _____

_____   _____

_____   _____

Interests: _____   Interests: _____

_____   _____

_____   _____

Notes: _____

_____

_____

_____

_____

_____

_____

_____

Student Daily Checklist—Teaming Competitions

Student Daily Checklist

Group (Strengths & Buddy Clusters):

Instructional Unit _____

Daily Tally:

Date	Total	Average

Name _____
_____ ( ) prepared ( ) participation
_____ ( ) prepared ( ) participation
_____ ( ) prepared ( ) participation
_____ ( ) prepared ( ) participation
_____ ( ) prepared ( ) participation
_____ ( ) prepared ( ) participation

Name _____
_____ ( ) prepared ( ) participation
_____ ( ) prepared ( ) participation
_____ ( ) prepared ( ) participation
_____ ( ) prepared ( ) participation
_____ ( ) prepared ( ) participation
_____ ( ) prepared ( ) participation

Name _____
_____ ( ) prepared ( ) participation
_____ ( ) prepared ( ) participation
_____ ( ) prepared ( ) participation
_____ ( ) prepared ( ) participation
_____ ( ) prepared ( ) participation
_____ ( ) prepared ( ) participation

Name _____
_____ ( ) prepared ( ) participation
_____ ( ) prepared ( ) participation
_____ ( ) prepared ( ) participation
_____ ( ) prepared ( ) participation
_____ ( ) prepared ( ) participation
_____ ( ) prepared ( ) participation

Name _____
_____ ( ) prepared ( ) participation
_____ ( ) prepared ( ) participation
_____ ( ) prepared ( ) participation
_____ ( ) prepared ( ) participation
_____ ( ) prepared ( ) participation
_____ ( ) prepared ( ) participation

Name _____
_____ ( ) prepared ( ) participation
_____ ( ) prepared ( ) participation
_____ ( ) prepared ( ) participation
_____ ( ) prepared ( ) participation
_____ ( ) prepared ( ) participation
_____ ( ) prepared ( ) participation

A Quick-Check System

Literacy Bin Activities

<u>A</u> = Accurate _____

<u>Q</u>uick = Quality Work _____

<u>C</u>heck = Complete _____

A Quick-Check System

Literacy Bin Activities

<u>A</u> = Accurate _____

<u>Q</u>uick = Quality Work _____

<u>C</u>heck = Complete _____

A Quick-Check System

Literacy Bin Activities

<u>A</u> = Accurate _____

<u>Q</u>uick = Quality Work _____

<u>C</u>heck = Complete _____

A Quick-Check System

Literacy Bin Activities

<u>A</u> = Accurate _____

<u>Q</u>uick = Quality Work _____

<u>C</u>heck = Complete _____

Note: A form can be distributed to groups of students to launch ideas and discussions. Once ideas are discussed and agreed upon, you can create a poster to display in your classroom.

Literacy Bin Observation Form

Literacy Bin Observation on _____ **Date** _____

Demonstrates appropriate behavior ( ) Yes   ( ) No

Selects Activities Appropriately ( ) Yes   ( ) No

Appropriate Pacing ( ) Yes   ( ) No

Works Well in Teams & Independently ( ) Yes   ( ) No

Self-Sufficient ( ) Yes   ( ) No

Comments _____

_____

_____

Literacy Bin Observation Form

Literacy Bin Observation on _____ **Date** _____

Demonstrates appropriate behavior ( ) Yes   ( ) No

Selects Activities Appropriately ( ) Yes   ( ) No

Appropriate Pacing ( ) Yes   ( ) No

Works Well in Teams & Independently ( ) Yes   ( ) No

Self-Sufficient ( ) Yes   ( ) No

Comments _____

_____

_____

Literacy Bin Portfolio Checklist

_____'s Literacy Bin Portfolio Checklist

Bin _____   Date _____

The work I've selected for my portfolio is:

( ) Accurate, Quality Work, Complete!

( ) Represents my Best Efforts!

( ) Unique—there's no activity like it in my portfolio!

( ) Work That Makes Me Proud!

I wanted to share this work because:

_____

_____

_____

Literacy Bin Portfolio Checklist

_____'s Literacy Bin Portfolio Checklist

Bin _____   Date _____

The work I've selected for my portfolio is:

( ) Accurate, Quality Work, Complete!

( ) Represents my Best Efforts!

( ) Unique—there's no activity like it in my portfolio!

( ) Work That Makes Me Proud!

I wanted to share this work because:

_____

_____

_____

Penny for Your Thoughts Survey

Name _____   Date_____

A Penny For Your Thoughts

On the _____ Mini Book Club!

1. List the strategies you practiced during the Mini Book Club:

_____

_____

_____

_____

Which strategy was the most challenging for you?_____

Which strategy was the least challenging for you?_____

2. Do you feel using these strategies helped you with your comprehension?

_____

_____

_____

3. Did you enjoy working with others? Do you feel the group was successful helping one another?

_____

_____

_____

4. What did you enjoy most about this Mini Book Club?

_____

_____

_____

5. What changes would you make to the next Mini Book Club?

_____

_____

_____

Personal Writing Plan for Monitoring

Personal Writing Plan

Name _____ Date _____

So Far, I Have Written:

1. _____

2. _____

3. _____

4. _____

5. _____

6. _____

7. _____

8. _____

Good Points About My Writing	Ways to Improve My Writing

Notes:

Daily Plan—Guided Reading

The following activities were covered or assigned during our Guided Reading instruction today (check = completed; no check = still to completed)

Date:

Reading Assignments & Activities	Effort
Written Response	Effort
Vocabulary	Effort
Other:	Effort

Comments:

Note: You may wish to modify this Daily Plan to align with your reading instruction and/or your student's needs.

Daily Plan—Guided Writing

Name: _____ Date: _____

Guided Plan for Writing: _____

Assignment: _____

Effort: _____

Time: _____

_____ **Read/Restate Task**	Time: _____ Date: _____
Planning	Time: _____ Date: _____
Break ☺	
Writing _____ **Intro**	Time: _____ Date: _____
_____ P { T 1. 2. 3. C	Time: _____ Date: _____
Break ☺	
_____ P { T 1. 2. 3. C	Time: _____ Date: _____
Break ☺	
_____ P { T 1. 2. 3. C	Time: _____ Date: _____
_____ **Conclusion//Intro**	Time: _____ Date: _____

Note: You may wish to modify this Daily Plan to align with your writing instruction and/or your student's needs.

Student Plan for Projects with Literacy Activities

Name_____ Plan Date: _____

Type of Project _____ Start Date _____ End Date _____

Activity	Plans & Estimated Date to Complete	Ability to Work Well With Others or Independently	Parent/Teacher Check

Incentives _____

_____

_____

Note: You may wish to modify this Plan to align with your instruction and/or your student's needs.

Broad Student Plan—Version 1

_____'s Daily Progress (* 2 points each)

Morning

_____ Assignment notebook signed by parent/homework completed/ materials in school

_____ Completed all class assignments appropriately

_____ Attentive and on-task

_____ Showed best effort on all work and made up any missed work (music lesson etc.)

_____ Participated well and worked well with others

_____/10

Afternoon

_____ Completed all class assignments appropriately

_____ Attentive and on-task

_____ Showed best effort on all work and made up any missed work (music lesson etc.)

_____ Participated well and worked well with others

_____ Assignment notebook filled-in and materials prepared for home

_____/10

Total _____

16–20 Very Good Day (full privileges)

11–15 Good Day (partial privileges)

10–0 Difficult Day (restricted privileges)

Broad Student Plan—Version 2

**At the end of every day, I will check to make sure I have all of my homework.
I will bring home all folders I need together with my Take Home Folder.**

_____ Assignment notebook was signed by parent/homework completed/material in school

_____ Completed all class assignments appropriately

	Monday	Tuesday	Wednesday	Thursday	Friday
Math					
ELA					
Science					
Social Studies					
Other					

Comments:

Student Contract

Name _____   Date_____

Contract for Increasing Effort

1. Do you feel you are as successful as you could be with your guided-reading activities?

_____
_____
_____

2. Are there areas you feel you could improve if you used more effort?

_____
_____
_____

3. What is your plan for using more effort to improve these areas? (How will you do it? When will you do it?)

_____
_____
_____

4. How can I or other people at school help you be successful with your plan?

_____
_____
_____

5. What are some fair consequences that you should face if you choose not to follow your plan?

_____
_____
_____

6. What are some rewards you would like to receive if you choose to follow your plan?

_____
_____
_____

_____   _____
(Student Signature)   (Teacher Signature)

References

Athans, S.K., & Ashe-Devine, D. (2008). *Quality comprehension: A strategic model of reading instruction using Read-Along Guides, grades 3–6.* Newark, DE: International Reading Association.

Athans, S., Clarke, J., Devine, D., & Sammon, K. (2005). *Guided reading assessment strategies: Classroom research.* East Syracuse, NY: Central New York Teaching Center.

Athans, S., Devine, D., Henry, D., Parente, R., & Sammon, K. (2006). *Motivation matters! Improving reading comprehension results: Classroom research.* East Syracuse, NY: Central New York Teaching Center.

Breaux, A., & Whitaker, T. (2006). *Seven simple secrets: What the best teachers know and do!* Larchmont, NY: Eye On Education.

Diller, D. (2005). *Practice with purpose: Literacy work stations for grades 3–6.* Portland, ME: Stenhouse.

Donahue, P.L., Daane, M.C., & Yin, Y. (2005). *The nation's report card: Reading 2003* (Publication No. NCES 2004–453). Washington, DC: U.S. Government Printing Office.

Fountas, I.C., & Pinnell, G.S. (1996). *Guided reading: Good first teaching for all children.* Portsmouth, NH: Heinemann.

Fountas, I.C., & Pinnell, G.S. (2001). *Guiding readers and writers, grades 3–6: Teaching comprehension, genre, and content literacy.* Portsmouth, NH: Heinemann.

Fountas, I.C., & Pinnell, G.S. (2002). *Leveled books for readers grades 3–6: A companion volume to guiding readers and writers.* Portsmouth, NH: Heinemann.

Fountas, I.C., & Pinnell, G.S. (2006). *The Fountas & Pinnell leveled book list, K–8.* Portsmouth, NH: Heinemann.

Gambrell, L.B., Palmer, B.M., Codling, R.M., & Mazzoni, S.A. (1996). Assessing motivation to read. *The Reading Teacher, 49,* 518–533.

Gambrell, L.B. (2007, May). *Strategy-based instruction.* Breakfast meeting sponsored by Sundance/Newbridge at the annual convention of the International Reading Association, Toronto, ON, Canada.

Gardner, H. (1983). *Frames of mind: The theory of multiple intelligences.* New York: Basic Books.

Guthrie, J.T., & Wigfield, A. (1997). *Reading engagement: Motivating readers through integrated instruction.* Newark, DE: International Reading Association.

Harness, C. (1999). *The Amazing Impossible Erie Canal.* New York: Aladdin Picture Books.

Harvey, S., & Goudvis, A. (2000). *Strategies that work: Teaching comprehension to enhance understanding.* York, ME: Stenhouse.

Kajder, S.B. (2006). *Bringing the outside in: Visual ways to engage reluctant readers.* Portland, ME: Stenhouse.

Karchmer, R.A., Mallette, M.H., Kara-Soteriou, J., & Leu, D., Jr. (Eds.). (2005). *Innovative approaches to literacy education: Using the Internet to support new literacies.* Newark, DE: International Reading Association.

Keene, E. (2006). *Assessing comprehension thinking strategies.* Huntington Beach, CA: Shell Education.

Keene, E., & Zimmerman, S. (2007). *Mosaic of thought: Second edition.* Portsmouth, NH: Heinemann.

Mendler, A.N. (2000). *Motivating students who don't care: Successful techniques for educators.* Bloomington, IN: Solution Tree.

Pearson, D., & Gallagher, M. (1983). The instruction of reading comprehension. *Contemporary Educational Psychology, 8*(3), 317–344.

Sagor, R. (2003). *Motivating students and teachers in an era of standards.* Alexandria, VA: Association for Supervision and Curriculum Development.

Slavin, R.E. (1994). *Using student team learning* (4th ed.). Baltimore: Johns Hopkins Team Learning Project.

Stix, A., & Hrbek, F. (2006). *Teachers as classroom coaches: How to motivate students across the content areas.* Alexandria, VA: Association for Supervision and Curriculum Development.

Tomlinson, C.A. (2001). *How to differentiate instruction in mixed-ability classrooms.* Alexandria, VA: Association for Supervision and Curriculum Development.

Willingham, D.T. (2007). Critical thinking: Why is it so hard to teach? *American Educator, 31*(2), 8–19.

Willingham, D.T. (2006/2007). The usefulness of brief instruction in reading comprehension strategies. *American Educator, 30*(4), 39–50.